Strategies for Raising Honest Children

STANDING UP AGAINST THE ODDS

ROBERT and DEBRA BRUCE

ELLEN OLDACRE

CPH.
SAINT LOUIS

Cover illustration by Mark Bender.

Scripture quotations, unless otherwise indicated, are taken from the HOLY BIBLE, NEW INTERNATIONAL VERSION®. NIV®. Copyright © 1973, 1978, 1984 by International Bible Society. Used by permission of Zondervan Publishing House. All rights reserved.

Quotations marked KJV are from the King James or Authorized Version of the Bible.

Biblical references marked RSV are from the Revised Standard Version of the Bible, copyrighted 1946, 1952, © 1971, 1973. Used by permission.

Verses marked TLB are taken from THE LIVING BIBLE, © 1971 by Tyndale House Publishers, Wheaton, IL. Used by permission.

Copyright © 1999 Concordia Publishing House

3558 S. Jefferson Avenue, St. Louis, MO 63118-3968

Manufactured in the United States of America

Library of Congress Cataloging-in-Publication Data
Bruce, Robert G., 1949–
    Standing up against the odds : strategies for raising honest
children / Robert and Debra Bruce and Ellen Oldacre.
        p. cm.
        ISBN 0-570-05377-3
        1. Child rearing—Religious aspects—Christianity. 2. Virtues.
I. Bruce, Debra Fulghum, 1951– II. Oldacre, Ellen W. III. Title
BV4529 .B785 2000
248.8′45—dc21   99-043447

1 2 3 4 5 6 7 8 9 10   08 07 06 05 04 03 02 01 00 99

To our children
Rob, Claire, Brittnye,
and Ashley

Stuart and Emily

ACKNOWLEDGMENTS

*We are extremely thankful to some very
talented people who believed in this book
and put their lives on hold to help us finish
it in a timely fashion, including:*

John Oldacre

J.R. Cunningham

Darrell Trout

The staff at ParentLife *and* Living with
Teenagers *magazines*

*We are also grateful to the staff at
Concordia Publishing House for realizing
the urgency of this book and working
overtime to get it to the public.*

CONTENTS

INNOCENCE LOST

The year was 1993. The place was the 52nd Inaugural Gala in Washington, D.C. in honor of President Bill Clinton. Touted as "An American Reunion," popular celebrities such as Michael Jackson, Fleetwood Mac, and Barbra Streisand entertained more than 18,000 guests on the premises, along with millions of television viewers. The program was perfectly planned—Hollywood at its best. Yet it was the words in Streisand's last song that captured the attention of millions. Her song? "Children Will Listen" from the Broadway musical, *Into the Woods*.

As Streisand blew a kiss to the cheering crowd, the final words of the song, "Careful before you say, 'Listen to me.' Children will listen ..." remained in the minds of many. Of course, who knew then that on August 17, 1998, President Bill Clinton would face a federal grand jury to answer questions about having an extramarital affair—in the Oval Office—with a female subordinate young enough to be his daughter.

A National Paralysis

From the day Bill Clinton took the oath of President of the United States, he became our nation's top leader. He went from being an ordinary citizen to our highest role model and chief representative of our great nation. Why do we hold our president in highest esteem? Because we elected him with great confidence to hold our nation in highest esteem! We address him as "Mr. President," and when he enters a room, we all stand out of reverence and respect for what he represents. Overseas, the president exemplifies our nation; his actions and reactions speak for America.

When President Clinton confirmed what most of us knew—that he had an "improper relationship" with the young White House intern—it was a moment of national paralysis. After months of trying to blame everyone else, this affirmation of the truth forced us to reassess our values and personal standards.

In his 1994 State of the Union Address, President Clinton expressed great alarm at the breakup of the family over the past 20 years. Blending inspiration with determination, President Clinton challenged Americans to change, saying, "The American people have got to want to change from within if we are going to bring back work, family, church, and community. Let's give our children a future. Let us take away their guns and give them books. Let us overcome despair and replace it with hope. Let us, by our example, teach them to obey the law, respect our neighbors, and cherish our values. Let us weave these sturdy threads into a new American community that once more can stand strong against the forces of despair and evil because everybody has a chance to walk into a better tomorrow."[1]

In 1994, President Clinton called for Americans to turn back to such high virtues as obedience, respect, and cherished values. He challenged communities to stand strong against the forces of evil. Yet four years later, our "pro-family-values president" is in trouble because of poor moral decisions. But of even greater concern: America is in trouble.

Who Will Lead Our Children?

From athletes to super models to politicians, the media constantly bombard us with the glitz and glamour of today's celebrities. Yet how many of these stars have become revered role models for our children? Perhaps too many. Polls indicate that unlike generations past, today's childhood role models are not those who have morally shaped our nation or biblical heroes. Rather, children lean toward celebrities who entertain us. This admiration of entertainers could be a clear indication that our society is morally adrift—we are led by an "image," not a true hero.

And what about sports heroes? There are some excellent Christian role models for our children in the athletic arena. Yet there still are many who are notorious for living flamboyant, secular lifestyles. Take basketball player Dennis Rodman, for example. It's hard to see Rodman's athletic talent as he appears on the court with electric hair colors, multiple tatoos, body piercings, and drag costumes. Though he has been suspended for head-butting a referee and kicking a courtside photographer, Rodman still calls the shots with his team, the media, and his millions of fans. Likewise, boxer Mike Tyson's numerous run-ins with the law have done nothing to dampen his popularity with children who were once enthralled with his muscular brawn and mighty blows.

If we can't always look to athletes for role models, what about "moral" leaders? Can we look to Rev. Henry Lyons, the former president of the National Baptist Convention U.S.A., who was convicted in 1999 of racketeering and grand theft? What about former Arkansas Governor Jim Guy Tucker, who in the midst of the Whitewater probe pleaded guilty to a tax evasion conspiracy charge?

Obviously, our children cannot glean the highest morals and values from some of our revered leaders. A recent study of college students revealed that of those questioned, only 5 percent think that most politicians are honest.[2] Contrast this to your impression of political officials when you were a child. Twenty years ago, most of us held the president in highest esteem and wanted to mimic the valued attributes of honesty, integrity, and truth.

While our perception of public officials has changed dramatically, one thing has not changed: the virtues laid out for us in the Bible. The country's willingness to overlook the choices of lying and adultery made by the president means many do not hold high the importance of fidelity, honesty, and respect. And looking beyond the Oval Office, other symptoms show a nation in trouble: elementary school shootings by young children, the high rate of sexually transmitted diseases among teenagers, middle school children using the impotence drug Viagra to help them perform sexually, and the widespread use of illicit drugs in all types of communities, to name a few.

In his book *Right from Wrong*, Josh McDowell attests to the problem with entrusting the development of our children's value systems to the masses: "The government says the solution is better education; they say more prevention programs will make a better society. Educators say the solution is more money; if we pour more money into our schools, we'll produce better kids. Activists say the solution is justice; they contend more police, more corporal punishment, more prisons, more job opportunities, more social programs."[3]

McDowell maintains that although many of the above are good goals, they don't address the root cause— our children are being raised in a society that "largely rejects the notions of truth and morality." In 1994, with the cooperation of 13 evangelical denominations, McDowell's organization, under the direction of the George Barna Research Group, conducted a survey with randomly selected youth groups across the United States and Canada. More than 3,700 youth answered their questionnaire. Even though these kids were actively involved in church activities and overwhelmingly identified their parents as loving, the survey showed that large numbers were involved in "inappropriate, immoral, or illegal behavior." In just the three months prior to the survey:

- *Two out of every three (66 percent) lied to a parent or other adult.*
- *Six in ten (59 percent) lied to their peers.*

- *One in three (36 percent) cheated on an exam.*
- *Nearly one in four (23 percent) smoked a cigarette.*
- *One in nine (12 percent) had gotten drunk.*

Judging from McDowell's poll, it becomes increasingly apparent that America's moral values are at an all-time low. What has happened? Have we become immune to the lies, manipulative tactics, and lack of ethics that brand many leaders in our nation—sadly, even some Christian leaders? Or have we merely sold out to the MTV Generation's "no absolutes" value system?

If you think this is overreacting, turn on your TV tonight. Or glance into your den while your teenagers are gathered with friends, watching TV. It's the shows you don't normally see that will shock you. Perhaps Madonna started the "mainstream" porn trend with her "Erotica" CD and her infamous *Sex* book. Today rapper Foxy Brown appears almost daily on MTV, as the star of pornographic movies, complete with her chrome bikini, as she bumps and grinds and makes erotic gestures in her popular video—and children as young as early elementary age watch and learn from her. Film clips from the movie *Eyes Wide Shut* are liberally shown during family viewing hours, showing actors Tom Cruise and Nicole Kidman making love before a full-length mirror. And children are watching.

Are we in a hopeless situation? No. But it is up to today's parents to make a change. As we are told in Ephesians 6:4, "Fathers, do not exasperate your children; instead, bring them up in the training and instruction of the Lord." It is our responsibility as parents to help our children grow in commitment to the eight values outlined in this book. We teach our children that some things are negotiable and others are not. Play time, eating dessert, curfews, clothes, and allowances are all negotiable and based on responsible age appropriateness. But more important for our children to learn is that God never changes. His Word is truth; it is rock solid. But He changes us through the Gospel and that is what motivates us to want to keep His commands.

A Hurried Society

America's apathy toward honesty and integrity indicates a far graver problem than any poll can indicate. The vast decline in America's morals and core values has left both parents and children confused. In the past two decades, America has become a "child-centered society," yet we have given our children no strong rules to live by.

In keeping with the hurried society we live in, we easily make babies, then concede to virtual parenting, allowing others to raise them soon after birth. We ask our preschoolers to make choices way too early, and set weak limits and boundaries for our teenagers. Then, we don't follow through with consequences if the rules are broken. Because the position of the family as central to American life has given way to the rights of the individual, parents have relinquished their authority to day care centers, schools, or even the government for fear of infringing upon those rights.

Consider how many well-meaning parents expect classroom teachers to teach their children about sex and morals through required sex education programs in public schools. Or what about those who allow the media—television, newspaper, popular magazines, and movies—to teach their children about life and love? Many parents expect the church to teach their children about Christianity, faith, and values. Yet these same parents wonder what happened when their children go astray, placing the blame everywhere except at home. As parents, we need to be aware of the "trickle down" effect that happens when we don't address such issues directly in the home.

A Wake-Up Call

This book offers the truth of God's Word, the power of the Gospel of forgiveness, which moves us to seek and live according to God's truth. In this book, you will find inspiring biblical truths that challenge us to seek and live according to God's Word. You will find proven and practical methods to help you teach your children to grow in the godliness that flows from a growing trust in Jesus. Family problems date back to biblical times but today's families face unique situations. No matter what the make-up of your home—a traditional family, two working parents, a single parent, stepparents, a grandparent raising grandchildren, or some other situation—you can learn to take charge of your family's faith development as you seek to know God, trust in His truth, and, led by Him, map out a solid plan to teach the following eight values:

- *Integrity*
- *Faithfulness*

- *Self-discipline*
- *Accountability*
- *Contentment*
- *Benevolence*
- *Forgiveness*
- *Hope*

The Parents Shall Lead

It is not enough to teach one or a few of these values. All are important because they are based on Christ's teachings in the Bible. This book will show you how to start right where you are and make immediate life changes as you work toward developing a Christlike code of behavior in your home in the midst of society's secular standards. The call to families is urgent, but the plea is that these values not be taught out of legalism based on fear and panic. Rather, we can depend on the amazing love that God Himself gives us in Jesus: "This is how God showed His love among us: He sent His one and only Son into the world that we might live through Him. This is love: not that we loved God, but that He loved us and sent His Son as an atoning sacrifice for our sins" (1 John 4:9–10). *His* love for us motivates us to want to make a difference.

Our children will face moral issues the rest of their lives. The lessons we teach them from God's Word are timeless and will serve them for years to come. This book will show you a unique method of teaching these lessons—a simple method called *Values Check* that will easily work in your home regardless of your children's ages. Originally, this method was used in a local church to train youth leaders and to ensure that adults were well-prepared before tackling the job as leader, teacher, or counselor. But the *Values Check* system is also highly effective in teaching values to children and teens.

Using such tools as family discussion, one-on-one conversation, role plays, question and answer, and consequences as rules are broken, parents can set the stage at home to teach these eight crucial values while children observe, learn, and act.

Each chapter incorporates the following three steps:

Values Check

Step 1: I Lead, You Follow

Step 2: You and I Lead Together

Step 3: You Lead, I Follow

The Time Is Right

In the following pages, you will be challenged to start today—right where you are—to change America's complacency by lifting high the noble attributes of honesty, ethics, and high personal standards in your home. By doing so, you can raise children who take pride in telling the truth, hold in highest esteem their family's honor, and make wise choices.

Train a child in the way he should go,
and when he is old he will not turn from it.
Proverbs 22:6

INTEGRITY

It is the soul that makes a nation great or small, noble or ignoble, weak or strong. It is the soul that exalts it to happiness, or sinks it to misery ... it is the spiritual side of humanity ... The life of the nation is secure only when the nation is honest, truthful, and virtuous: for upon these conditions depend the life of its life.

Frederick Douglass, on the 23rd anniversary of Emancipation (1885)

Truth Means Trust

For you to pick up this book shows that you have some concern about the status and well-being of your treasure, the family; it means that honesty and integrity are important to you. Nonetheless, are you striving to teach values that will enable your child to grow into an honest Christian adult—one who believes in right and wrong? We are talking about the core values that are accepted as "right" by Judaism and every Christian denomination—the values given by God Himself, summarized in the Ten Commandments. They are spelled out in Exodus 20 and summarized by Jesus: " 'Love the Lord your God with all your heart and with all your soul and with all your mind.' This is the first and greatest commandment. And the second is like it: 'Love your neighbor as yourself.' All the Law and the Prophets hang on these two commandments" (Matthew 22:37–40). In that light, let's define morality as obedience to God. Because of what God has done for us through Jesus' death and resurrection, we will make choices in life that reflect our love for Him.

Truth means trust. It reports what actually occurred without leaving out facts or fabricating imaginary facts.

Rabbi Wayne Dosick describes the truth succinctly, "The reality is, if we tell the truth, we only have to tell the truth once. If you lie, you have to keep lying forever."[4] While we want to be able to hold those in the public eye accountable to the truth, that is not always possible. We cannot control what others say or do. Nonetheless, we can hold ourselves and our families accountable as we encourage the highest integrity in the Christian home. Integrity means being "complete" or "whole," and is synonymous with honor or honesty. It is this message that we teach our children.

Standing Tall

The cost of being a Christian in a secular world is high. Yet God asks us to do things that take a great deal of courage and that may be painful. Especially when faced with conflicting values, it is important to know that standing strong or having integrity is what Christians are to do—even though it is not always easy. The good news is that no matter what the past holds, we all can celebrate a "spiritual renewal" in our homes. God's forgiveness and grace give us hope to begin a life of high integrity as we live and model biblical values for our children.

A Scottish poet once said, "If I have been privileged to catch a more comprehensive glimpse of life than many other men, it is because I have stood on the shoulders of my parents." The truth of the matter is that all children stand on the shoulders of their parents. The straighter, taller, and truer parents stand, the better the view of life their children will have. Standing tall with integrity means that you lift high such noble traits as honesty and strength of character. While it may seem like an awesome thought, your child perceives you to have the highest integrity of anyone he or she knows. Even if teens rebel during adolescence, those seeds of faith you plant by teaching values such as integrity eventually come to maturity.

Lean on God's Word

"For as he thinketh in his heart, so is he."
Proverbs 23:7 KJV

We've all heard the expression, *Says who?* at some time when raising children, especially as they approach the teenage years. Perhaps the most startling comeback is, "God says!" God gave us a code for living: The Ten Commandments. After all, Moses did not bring down the Ten Suggestions from Mount Sinai, he brought down a universal code for human behavior—from that moment until the end of time. The Ten Commandments describe

God's will for our lives. Having been saved and touched by His love, we want to know and seek that will.

Each commandment teaches us in a straightforward manner how to relate to God and to our neighbors. The first commandments deal with our relationship with our Creator. " 'I am the LORD, your God, who brought you out of the land of Egypt, out of the house of bondage. You shall have no other gods before Me. You shall not make for yourself a graven image ... You shall not take the name of the LORD your God in vain ... Observe the Sabbath day, to keep it holy" (Deuteronomy 5:6–12 RSV). The remaining commandments deal with our relationship with others: " 'Honor your father and your mother ... You shall not kill. Neither shall you commit adultery. Neither shall you steal. Neither shall you bear false witness against your neighbor. Neither shall you covet' " (Deuteronomy 5:16–21 RSV).

As you model and teach the Ten Commandments to your child, realize that for the Christian they are more liberating than enslaving, and they are extremely relevant to our nation today. The Commandments speak about adultery and accountability. They say that we cannot worship more than one God, that we must not misuse the power God entrusts to us to harm others, that we must maintain life in community by avoiding certain kinds of conduct that will simply—over time—destroy life in community. They also require us to think about what we are to do about those who take life, break the marriage vows, or claim for themselves the lives and goods of other people.

Inner Strength

Studies show that faith in God, trusting in His unchanging Word, provides inner strength and support to children, especially during the tumultuous adolescent years. In more than 100 studies, there was a significant correlation between the acceptance of traditional moral values and moral restraint.

Values Check

I Lead, You Follow

Remember, parents have the highest integrity rating of anyone a young child knows—so watch what you do! Use teachable moments to reinforce the traits of integrity:

- *Talk about someone you know who has high integrity. Explain honesty, high personal standards, and values using words your child can understand.*

- *Read the Ten Commandments to your child, and discuss them in simple terms. Talk about the consequences for such acts as stealing, lying, or cheating.*

- *Encourage your child to become "inner directed"—to act according to God's will instead of what is most popular at the moment. We do not take a Gallup poll to determine right behavior for a situation. The majority does not rule on what is ethical. Instead, we have the indwelling Spirit of the living God as our barometer. And we remember God's love for us in Christ for the power to do what is right.*

You and I Lead Together

- *At the grocery store, let your child help you push the cart back to the appropriate place instead of leaving it in the parking lot.*

- *Let your child motion for someone to get in front of you while waiting in a long line at the bank.*

- *Together, pick up clothes that have fallen from the rack at the department store, and let your child help you hang them back up—even if you didn't knock them off!*

- *Pick up trash on the sidewalk at church and find a nearby trash can.*

You Lead, I Follow

As your child grows in wisdom and years, stay on top of how he handles peer situations and guide him in a commitment to living a life of integrity.

- *Praise your child for telling the truth even if he has to pay the consequences with parents, friends, or teachers.*

- *Affirm your child when she is firm with her standards around friends.*

- *Stand by his side when your child says no to persuasive friends who try to get him into uncomfortable situations.*

Strengthen Christian Values

Everyone's talking about "family values" today. But over the past 10 years, the standards most people have held dear to their hearts have rapidly eroded across our nation. Teaching personal standards in the home is not an easy task these days, especially when your child is bombarded by the media's view of right and wrong.

The family provides our first understanding of traditional ethical values and personal standards, providing a safe "testing ground" for our children. Within the nest of this accepting group of people, your child will experiment with all sorts of rebellious behavior, testing to see what will be approved and what will be disapproved.

The Greatest Role Model

Your child will learn Christian values by watching you act and react in the world. Remember that Jesus is our great role model. We touch the lives of our children the most when they see us taking Jesus at His Word and living as He taught us. The ways you show caring to others will give that important pattern that your child will slowly pick up and establish in her own life. How you handle neighbor relationships, family matters, and giving in your community reinforces your personal integrity. As children learn to resolve conflict without physical violence, to treat others compassionately, and to choose right over wrong, they will take these behaviors into their school and neighborhood, and ultimately into their own families and society.

A Personal Note

With a college freshman and two young adults in our house, perhaps the most frequent expression we've heard during the past few years is, "But everybody else does this." Or "Joe's dad lets him go." How do we respond? By asserting: We aren't everyone else. In our home we don't do that.

When your teens complain about your family's strong personal standards, use it as an opportunity to explain why your family does not go to certain movies or watch questionable television shows. Tell them why your family does not use vulgar language or wear some clothes they may be attracted to in mass market magazines. Most important, affirm what is right and good about your family—about your teens—and the personal standards you have chosen to follow. Read to them from the Bible and let them see the verses you select that challenge Christians to decency, high standards, and Christlike values and behavior.

Bob

Stand Up for Honesty

Parenthood is working with God in molding and shaping the future of your child. Part of shaping character is teaching honesty. Yet being honest is a very strange thing. If your child is too honest, people will accuse him of being rude, blunt, and inconsiderate. Then, when he hides his real feelings and tells people what they want to hear, people may think he is phony and insincere. Should he ever give his honest opinion?

Psychologists tell us that people who are secure and happy with themselves have no need to put others down. A sign of security and maturity is the ability to develop a positive relationship in which there is mutual support. There is a big difference between positive critique and negative criticism. Honesty is certainly an important element in positive relationships. But how and why honest words are spoken is just as important.

While your child's outright lies may stem from fantasies or fears, it is important to always get back to basics—what really is truth. Your child may have an over-active imagination as Rob did when he blamed all his wrongdoings on his imaginary pals, Ready, Roddy, and Rudy. His parents asked 4-year-old Rob if he messed up his toys after they were put away for the evening, and he stared them in the eyes and said, "Not me. It was Ready, Roddy, and Rudy." Of course, the imaginary tale was humorous at age 4, but if your 15-year-old is lying and throwing the blame elsewhere, you need a heart-to-heart confrontation!

A Personal Note

For years in our family we were frequently confronted with overly-assertive children who seemed to know all life's answers. When our son, Rob, was in third grade, he answered a visiting theology professor abruptly:

"And what will you be when you grow up?" the wise professor asked our son at a formal dinner. "Will you follow your father's footsteps and be a minister?"

And the honest but embarrassing truth was spoken.

"Actually, Dr. Burns," Rob spoke with great boyhood confidence, "I don't think so. The hours of a minister are much too long for me, and the pay scale is pretty low."

Another time, our middle daughter, Brittnye, blurted loudly at the "welcome dinner" in our newly-appointed church, "Whoever cooked this food sure can't cook!" We cringed as all eyes shot our way.

Of course, as parents, we have learned to sit back and let such childish remarks roll across our toughened skin, then discuss the matter later—behind closed doors. But what about training our children to be honest with their communication without being verbally abusive? Can it be done? Yes! Read on.

Deb

Values Check

I Lead, You Follow

- *Read the following Scripture verses to your child, and talk about the biblical guidelines for effective, loving communication: Ephesians 4:15, Ephesians 4:25, Philippians 4:8.*

- *Model honesty. When you do or say something wrong, admit it.*

- *No matter how trite, when you are faced with telling a "white lie," think about the repercussions. What may seem like an innocent white lie to you can give the impression of dishonesty to your child.*

- *Watch the excuses you give others. Don't say you cannot usher at church because you are ill when you are actually planning to play golf that day. Your children will see this for what it really is—untruth! Stay above board with what you say and do.*

You and I Lead Together

- *Help your child learn to note the difference between truth and opinion. Talk with your child and ask her to determine which is the truth and which is opinion. Talk together about statements she may make that are true and those that are just her opinion. In what ways can her opinion be hurtful to someone?*

* *Rob's bicycle is old and dirty. (opinion)*
* *Rob's bicycle is seven years old. (truth)*
* *Rene's shoes are torn. (truth)*
* *Rene's shoes are not very fashionable. (opinion)*
* *Mr. Baker is a mean father. (opinion)*
* *Mr. Baker makes his children go to bed at 7:00. (truth)*

* *Talk about the TV news or TV shows that may portray someone lying. Tell how this one lie affects many people and why it is wrong.*

You Lead, I Follow

As your child learns to speak the truth without hurting others, make sure he includes the following techniques in his speaking manner:

* *Avoid insults.*
* *Avoid labeling others.*
* *Be very specific when discussing a problem.*
* *Avoid using fatalistic language such as "this always happens."*
* *State the actual problem.*
* *Don't place blame.*
* *Avoid accusatory statements such as "you always ..." or "you never ..."*
* *Realize what is truth and what is opinion.*

Issue appropriate consequences for any dishonest behavior. The rules and consequences you give your child now will prepare him for following society's rules and consequences in years to come.

Encourage Tactfulness

Tact is that delicate perception of knowing the right thing to say or do without offending the other person. When a person uses tact in talking with others without distorting the truth in any way, growth happens. You use tact in relationships because you care about the other person and how he or she feels. This involves speaking the truth with hopes of preserving the friendship rather than tearing it apart.

Many times your child may be claiming to speak the truth when the idea is merely his own opinion or a judgment based on insufficient evidence. Statements such as, "My sister is really a brat" or "Her dress is ugly" are opinions, not truths.

Jesus Teaches a Better Way

In the gospels, Jesus teaches us a lifestyle that is full of empathy—one that is sensitive to those around us. This agape or selfless love He shares enables us to meet the personal needs of our family and friends, rather than tearing people down.

Helping our children develop into honest adults is one of our primary goals. But our children still must make their own judgments about what is truth and what is opinion. And children need to learn to measure truth and decide if what they say is going to hurt or destroy others.

The following questions can help your child learn to weigh judgments as she speaks or thinks and can help her determine that fine line between actual truth and opinion.

1. Ask, "What will my friend's reaction be?"

2. Ask, "Will the statement help the friend-ship grow?"

3. Ask, "What is my reason for speaking the truth?"

4. Ask, "Can I say the statement in a positive manner?"

5. Ask, "Will the statement still be true a week from now?"

Values Check

I Lead, You Follow

To equip our children with integrity, we all hold fast to Proverbs 22:6: "Train a child in the way he should go, and when he is old he will not turn from it." You can "train" your child as you:

- *Practice what you "preach" and model spirituality.*
- *Take a faith inventory and check your "internal" life.*
- *Share your personal faith in Jesus Christ.*
- *Get involved in a local church—together.*
- *Read the Bible with your child, explain how the Scriptures are meaningful today, and encourage a daily prayer time.*
- *Teach your child to look for God's love in all people and in all things each day.*
- *Teach your child the importance of an active prayer life.*
- *Go beyond teaching values by showing your child how to follow ways of love demonstrated by Jesus Christ.*

- *Root your child in the Christian faith so when he faces life's opposing influences, he has strength to persevere.*

You and I Lead Together

Using role plays, act out situations that call for your child to take a stand on unpopular but moral issues. You might use the following themes:

- *A new child is being made fun of at school.*
- *A friend asks to cheat off her paper.*
- *The teacher wrongly accuses a classmate.*
- *A team member uses the Lord's name in vain.*
- *A friend throws trash in the neighbor's yard.*

After the role play, talk about the outcome. How did your child act and react? Was it with integrity? What could he have done differently? How did it feel to stand up for something he believes in?

You Lead, I Follow

In this last step of teaching integrity, you will have to watch for times when your child makes personal decisions to have integrity with friends and family members. These may be from situations at school, on the soccer field, or at home. In any case, observe your child's words and actions; interject when necessary. If your child is not acting with integrity, help her learn from this experience by asking such questions as:

- *How would you feel if a friend did that to you?*
- *What do you think Jesus would do?*
- *Is this the best decision to make?*
- *What other choice might show integrity?*

Put Words into Action

Even though your child tells you, "Mom, I've heard that before," keep talking! You can never talk too much about integrity, for these lessons must be internalized in your child's head and heart. Even in the youngest child, feelings of compassion, fairness, and empathy can be experienced—if someone teaches them.

How can your child respond with integrity? He can

- *Stand up for a friend who is being treated unfairly.*
- *Refuse to gossip.*
- *Set the record straight when falsehoods are shared.*
- *Forgive someone who has offended or hurt him.*
- *Meet the needs of someone in class or in the neighborhood.*
- *Spend time in Bible study and prayer.*
- *Change a lifestyle that does not fit God's plan.*

It is in moments of temptation that we teach our children to stand firm and deal with the opposition head-on. While they cannot ignore the temptation or the peer who is luring them into worldly behavior, they can deal with it by saying no or confronting the person. Dealing with the potential sin may be difficult but the consequences of falling into sin are far worse.

Reinforcing Integrity with Youth

It is often difficult for elementary-age children and teenagers to stand up for what is right, especially when peers try to tear down what they believe. Perhaps you can remember what you were up against during your teenage years. But you also know that faith in Jesus provides us with courage to stand up to outside problems. This means that no matter what ethical issues your teen faces, as Christians we are summoned to live *in* the world, but not be *of* the world. We can experience an abundant life right where we are without giving in to society's demands.

Realize God Knows Our Feelings

No matter how rough the day is at home or school, it is important to know that God is there; He feels our pain and sorrow. Remind your child that while it's sometimes hard for us to tell the truth and stand up for what is right, God is in control. We don't always know why God places us where He does in life, but we do know that as difficult as our situations may be, He is with us and has a plan for us.

Record Personal Feelings

Encourage older children and teens to use a daily journal to record the events in their lives. This will take some soul-searching as they evaluate uncomfortable situations at school or play, identify their feelings, name spiritual experiences, and get in touch with how they personally act and react when confronted with unethical practices.

Lean on His Word for Strength

Paul gives words of advice, saying, "Follow my example, as I follow the example of Christ" (1 Corinthians 11:1). This practice is crucial for all of us as we try to nurture a spiritual journey in the home. Talk with your children and teens about how we work out physically by running, climbing stairs, swimming, and doing aerobics to get in touch with our body and to develop it. The same is true with spiritual disciplines such as Bible study, prayer, worship, and fellowship with other Christians. We do this to develop our relationship with God and one another. Acknowledging your faith in Jesus as Lord and Savior is the beginning of a personal relationship—a faith walk—with Him. Spiritual growth takes time just as physical growth; God works in the life of the believer in His own timing.

Become a "Principle-Centered" Christian

Author Stephen Covey presents a holistic approach for solving problems in *The Seven Habits of Highly Effective People* as he invites readers to become "principle centered." This means to stand apart from the emotion of the situation and from other factors that would act on you, and evaluate the options. "As a principle-centered person, you see things differently," Covey states. "And because you see things differently, you think differently, you act differently."[5]

To look at Covey's idea from a Christian perspective, you might instead say, "As a Christian, saved by God's grace and led by His Spirit, you see things differently. And because you see things differently, you think differently, you act differently." This statement encourages your child to seek God's will in every area of his life.

Share with your child or teen the following Scripture verse and talk about the high personal standards Christians seek: "Do not conform any longer to the pattern of this world, but be transformed by the renewing of your mind. Then you will be able to test and approve what God's will is—His good, pleasing and perfect will" (Romans 12:12).

Seek Opportunities to Share God's Love

Christ's love is others-centered. Because of His sacrifice for us, we reach out to others. As Christ-centered people, we don't live out our faith just at church or before close friends; we are called to share God's grace with all people. Challenge your child or teen to let those at school or play know he is a Christian through his behaviors of integrity such as generosity, gentleness, and honesty. These attributes will show that he is different—even though there may be conflict in relationships.

Affirm your child's integrity during rough times by sharing, "When you take a stand for what is right, it will be difficult. However, there are no guarantees that you will be insulated from the worst life has to offer. Just know that you are doing what is right, and God is with you."

Teach Your Children Well

Many would agree that Christian parents have a lot of catching up to do as the secular world crashes into our homes and seeks to destroy our personal standards. As a parent, you are your child's first teacher. Don't leave the moral and ethical development of your children up to schools or society. As you encourage spiritual development in your child, realize that you are the most important role model in her life. How you act, react, speak, and make choices in your everyday life will be interpreted by her and acted out in her own life.

A visitor to Mother Teresa's Calcutta mission was overwhelmed by the abject infirmity and poverty and asked, "How can you provide for all the hungry people who come to the mission?" The elderly nun's answer speaks to each of us of the ultimate responsibility we have in life: "One mouth at a time."

In the midst of scandals, lies, distrust, and dishonor that confront us every day, we still have the ultimate challenge to change the world—one child at a time. With Christ's help, let the value of integrity begin in your home, "one mouth at a time."

② FAITHFULNESS

A Personal Note

I watched the precocious 3-year-old in the airport terminal asking his parents a million questions. I could not help but continue to observe him on the airplane. His curiosity was magnetic. His mother used a matter-of-fact tone with him but her answers were not audible from my seat. However, his questioning inflection could be heard several seats down the row. He wanted to know about the normal kinds of things—the wing, the flight attendants, the propellers, and the buttons above him. But just as we climbed to our flying altitude and leveled off, he asked an amazing question. As if he was on a mid-air scouting expedition, he strained his head frantically looking from one window to the next and finally blurted out, "Where's God?" I knew exactly what he was thinking. Apparently, he had been told that God was in heaven, which was "up there." So when he finally got "up there," of course he expected to see God!

Ellen

We forget how literal children are. They expect us to be honest, especially when we talk to them about God. They ask questions about God out of their curious nature. They learn from us and store up what they hear and see as their adult role models live out a personal faith. As they approach adolescence and naturally want to find emotional and spiritual independence, they constantly check the answers received in childhood with what they are experiencing. The searching faith of teenagers screams with honesty. They not only test what they were told growing up, they add their own tests. They desperately want to know if God is true and honest. As parents and role models, we must continue to live out our faith honestly before them, but accept that they are searching for their own faith. We want them to become independently dependent upon God. Raising an honest child begins in helping your child understand the very nature of God—faithfulness. Knowing that the God who created her is the same yesterday, today, and tomorrow is foundational for your child. And, like it or not, our children will interpret God's faithfulness to them through our faithfulness to them.

Faithful to the Cause

Bill Clinton is an adult role model by nature of his role as president just as you are by nature of your role as parent. Our children need us to help them untangle all they have heard about the actions of a president who attends church, carries a Bible, and professes a faith in God. They will be confused by his misuse of presidential power. Regardless of what we think or feel about the president or his actions, we take ownership of the bottom line. As parents, teachers, and leaders, we are responsible for what we pass down to the children of the next century. We are the only ones who can really change any trickle-down effect of the president's immorality.

People do choose their own character, but children and teenagers need help sorting through the options and understanding the consequences. In her book *Preparing for Parenthood*, Dr. Grace Ketterman writes, "Being a good parent is not convenient. It is instead a constant challenge to avoid damaging extremes and to establish healthy balance. One of the core needs of every child is the need for consistency or predictability."[6] Ketterman stresses that proactive parenting "requires thinking, planning, and goal setting." She strongly encourages parents to decide what kind of character they want their child to have before he is even born. She suggests that if parents want a child who is tender and kind, then they must treat him gently but firmly so he will feel safe enough to give of himself to others.

God is faithful. And if we want our children to model the character of God, then we purposefully and powerfully teach them faithfulness as the beginning point of honesty. It is the rock of our Christian faith.

As our children grow, it becomes a greater challenge to remain faithful to the cause of raising an honest child. If you have teenagers, you know how that can happen.

Problem

Why do many parents throw in the towel just when the crucial adolescent years kick in?

Parenting is tiring business. If we don't keep a healthy balance in our own lives, we burn out before our children reach adolescence. Parents of young children need to be aware that parenthood lasts a long time. For years, their children's education will demand their time. Their children will be involved with on-going activities creating busy schedules on top of the parents' own busy schedules. Knowing how and when to say no and keeping yourself healthy require forethought and discipline.

Solution

- *Listen to your body. If you feel tired all the time, find out why. You will have to live with the way you treat your body now for the rest of your life. And you probably would like that to be a long life! So, guard your time and your health. Choose one good thing at a time in which to be involved.*

- *Realize that your most important job is parenting.*

- *Declare certain nights "family nights," allowing nothing else to interfere with the activity you and your family will do together.*

- *Listen to your child. If your child is consistently misbehaving or acting out, perhaps she is screaming for a slower pace and more of your attention.*

- *Pray without ceasing. Listen to God. God loves you and cares about you and your family. What was the sermon about last Sunday? What did someone you talked to tell you about God? What Scripture did you just happen to run across? See if there is a pattern. Is God trying to tell you something?*

Stop—Slow Down—Listen

Remember: The ones you are trying to be faithful to will help you know if you are missing the mark.

Are Parents Really Important?

You are always a parent but can you relieve yourself of feeling any responsibility for how your child turns out? Yes, by reading *The Nurture Assumption: Why Children Turn Out the Way They Do; Parents Matter Less Than You Think and Peers Matter More* by Judith Rich Harris. Harris contends that after donating an egg and sperm, nothing else parents do will influence their child's behavior. No parental words, hugs, encouragement, discipline, or influence make a difference. She adamantly writes that nothing parents do will affect a child's behavior, mental health, self-worth, or personality. Parents do not make the difference, according to Harris, peers do. If parents really want to do the best for their children, Harris suggests you make enough money to live in a good neighborhood so your children associate with the "right peers." Obviously, the author's decree relieves all parents from past, present, or future guilt. We don't need to be concerned over what we do or what we teach our children anymore. We just need to be sure they "hang out" with the right friends.

If we agreed with Harris' theory, we certainly wouldn't waste our time—or yours—with this book. Peers are indeed influential and important, but parents and the home environment ultimately have the most influence in a child's life. Yes, Mom and Dad—you *do* make a difference.

We have a parental mandate from God to "train up a child in the way he should go" and to teach our children spiritual truths. The Bible instructs us to raise our children in the nurture and admonition of the Lord, and as Christians, we know we are accountable for doing just that. Keep in mind that there are no guarantees. God never says, "Your children will always be perfect and turn out just as you have planned." He never says, "All children will grow up free of problems and never hurt their parents." Instead, He gives us the instructions, then promises to be with us in everything we do. Our parental calling is to trust and obey the God who created our children and entrusted them to our care.

Problem

Some parents assume they have done their part by the time adolescence rolls around. They sacrificed during the formative years and now, as their child approaches adolescence, they rest and let the church, the school, or peers take over the responsibility of teaching.

Solution

You can't throw in the towel, because you didn't have one to begin with. Parenting doesn't come with an "out." Oh, you can take a hiatus from it, but you will pay the price and even worse, so will your child. God calls you to a lifetime of parenting.

Part of your job is to know what everyone else is teaching your child or teenager. You might not want to give the job away to them just yet. Look through your child's or teen's textbooks. What do they say about religion, tolerance, or history? Is it what you believe? Get to know your child's teachers. Open your home to your teenager and his friends. Get to know them. Know what their strengths and weaknesses are. Be alert to their influences on your teen.

The nature of many decisions and discussions with an adolescent is serious, and the consequences carry lifelong effects. Couple this with the weight of helping your teen make good choices, while coping with her emotional ups and downs, and the task can be draining. This too shall pass. Do not take everything she says to you personally. Hang in with her. Discuss rules and privileges with her. If needed, write a contract with her that states what you both agree to and the consequences for irresponsibility.

Your influence on your child will be powerful and long-lasting. There is no greater cause than to faithfully parent a child. The journey is long and difficult, but the rewards are eternal.

No matter how many public figures come and go during your child's life, he will learn faithfulness to his family and his God from you. The 3-year-old Ellen observed on the airplane voiced what we all cry out at different times in our lives: "Where is God?" It's a good question. Our children need to know that it's all right to ask us anything, especially spiritual questions. Their faith begins at home. A church that loves them and supports them will offer experiences that grow their faith, but it is the home that sustains it. In *Experiencing God*, Henry Blackaby encourages readers to find out where God is working and join Him there. It is in the home that a child first begins to "experience God." Your child watches how you act and react to life and to him. He is looking to see if your actions and your words demonstrate that you know where God is and that you are faithful to Him.

Leave a Living Legacy

Many presidents have left legacies. When we think of Franklin Delano Roosevelt we recall fireside chats, the New Deal, and "All we have to fear is fear itself." We think of the military strategies of Dwight Eisenhower. History dubs the Kennedy years as Camelot and we remember John Kennedy saying, "Ask not what your country can do for you, but what you can do for your country." It remains to be seen what legacy history will attach to President Bill Clinton. It doesn't really matter. Ultimately, it is *your* legacy that will impact your children the most. What are you passing down to them that the world cannot take away? Is your example a living legacy of faithfulness to God that counters the lifestyles of less-than-admirable public personalities your children might hear about?

A Personal Note

I came straight from the airport to the surgery waiting room of the hospital in my hometown. It was as if I had stepped into a family reunion except only five of the 20 people there were related to me by blood or marriage. The rest were part of our family of faith. My dad was in six hours of surgery for five heart bypasses and our "family" had come to stand beside us just as my parents had done for so many of them through the years. Their faithfulness to God and to the friends who needed them spoke volumes to me. These were the people after whom I have modeled my life.

Each day as I traveled back and forth to the hospital from my parents' home, I passed by the church that helped raise me. The ministers, teachers, and volunteers wove their influence into the very fabric of who I am. They were faithful to God's call over the years to "train up a child." They provided me with a safe, loving laboratory to try out the gifts God had given me. Their faithful encouragement shaped my direction. There are not many villages who are faithful in raising their children. My church was.

Each night as I returned to my parents' home, I was surrounded by family pictures and reminders of the faith of my parents. The only item missing was my mom's Bible because she wanted it with her at the hospital. My dad came through the surgery in fine form.

My experience burned anew in my heart the need for parents to surround their children with examples of faithfulness.

Ellen

If you are thinking that the homes we were raised in or that our children have been raised in are perfect, don't! We have seen our share of pain, disappointments, divorce, depression, death, and mistakes. Faith is how we handle all the interruptions along the journey. But nothing can take away the legacy of faithfulness passed down to us. It is a gift. It is ours for all eternity for us to choose to use for strength for the journey. How could we give our children anything less? How can you? No matter who you are or who you aren't, or what your circumstances are, you can begin right now giving your children the most precious gift—a living legacy of faithfulness to your loving and faithful God.

Values Check

I Lead, You Follow

You know your child well because you spend time with him. You spend so much time with him, you create special memories with him that you will talk about for the rest of your life. You will pass these memories down to your grandchildren. God allows us to experience the same kind of relationship with Him.

- *Spending quiet time with God in Bible study and prayer helps you know Him.*
- *Reading the Bible gives you insights into God's character and His design for your life and your home.*
- *Getting to know God intimately gives us a purpose for the journey. And that purpose gives us a reason to care about what influences our children as they start their own journey.*

When your children are younger, it is difficult to find time alone because there is so much to be done. The good thing about God is He's always there. No matter how we feel or where we are, He's there. Your quiet time may consist of "road prayers" as you drive down the highway, or "oatmeal prayers" as you get breakfast ready for the family.

To maximize your time each day, pray for specific people and needs on specific days. Put Scripture verses or motivational quotes on cards and tape them to bathroom mirrors or car visors. Put them on the cabinets and the refrigerator to remind you and your family of God's Word.

A Thousand Words Are Worth a Picture

Your children are listening to you. They put together your words over their growing years and actually take on the attitudes you convey through your words. What do your words tell them about your feelings toward your family, your job, your church, your pastor, their school faculty, or your neighbors? Are you teaching them how to be faithful to God under all circumstances? Are they learning how their words and actions affect the lives of others?

Children believe that we will do what we say we will do. They put their complete trust in us. Through our example, they learn to trust that God keeps His promises. What are your children seeing?

You and I Lead Together

What does your child really know about God's faithfulness to you?

- *As you go through daily activities and interruptions, tell her how much God has done for you.*
- *Give God credit for major miracles and everyday small ones.*

- *Share with your child what you read in your quiet time. Let him know that your time alone with God is important to you.*

- *When you do something wrong that affects your child, let her hear you say, "I'm sorry." It will allow her to see that you are honest and faithful to being the best example you can be.*

- *Recount your own walk with Jesus with your child. If you have a spiritual heritage, make sure your child hears about it from you and from older generations.*

- *Pray without ceasing. Pray before meals. Try to have a special time once a week to sit down and pray as a family. Pray about family problems. Don't sweep them under the carpet in an attempt to protect your children.*

- *Acknowledge answered prayer. When you pray together, thank God for His faithfulness.*

- *Keep a list of prayer requests and answers to prayer in a family notebook.*

- *Pray for your child's friends and her friends' families.*

- *When you are in the car together, talk about God.*

- *Read books in which the main characters demonstrate faithfulness. Talk about the characters and the choices they make.*

- *Introduce your child to people you know who are faithful to what God has called them to do. Help your child to think of questions to ask them. Invite them into your home for a visit or a meal.*

- *Read and study about faithful Bible characters. Use age appropriate Bible storybooks. Be sure to include stories about the following: Noah, Paul, Abraham, David, Miriam, Isaiah, Moses, Jeremiah, Hannah, Elijah, Samuel, and Peter.*

The Bible doesn't leave out the difficult part of its characters' lives. Many of our faithful Bible heroes made mistakes with far-reaching consequences. But the Bible also records that after hearing their broken spirit of repentance, God forgave them and allowed them to be used again. It is important for children to understand that our attitude toward consequences, repentance, and forgiveness reflects our faithfulness toward God.

For the word of the LORD is right and true; He is faithful in all He does. Psalm 33:4

You Lead, I Follow

Catch your child being faithful and praise her. As you pray with her, thank God for her faithfulness. Be aware of areas where your child may need encouragement to remain faithful:

1. Does she keep her promises?

2. Is she dependable?

3. Does she do the right thing no matter what anyone else does?

4. Does she follow through with homework and household responsibilities without being reminded?

5. Does she finish what she starts?

Where There Is Confusion, There Is Opportunity

Opportunities to Clear Up the Facts

What has happened in the highest political office of our country is an outrage. As adults, we often allow our outrage to continue to swelter. We bombard our children with our angry opinions. They definitely need to understand the inappropriateness of our president's behavior, but rage alone has no positive result. Instead, turn your outrage into an opportunity.

Use events so graphically reported by the media as a time to answer honestly your child's questions about sex. Younger school-age children are not emotionally, intellectually, or physically mature enough to understand and cope with all the information. Answer their questions with concise, honest answers. Avoid telling them more than they need or want to know.

Some preteens and most teenagers are capable of handling more information and now is a very good time to make sure they know the correct facts about sex and all the issues involved. Take the opportunity to talk about the responsibility we have for the lives and well-being of others.

Your preteens and teenagers are beginning to understand the dangers of manipulation between the sexes and between all human beings. Discuss how men and women use and abuse power.

Help your children become aware of the draw of media-hype whether it is the truth or not. Point out statements that reek of sensationalism.

Opportunities to Give Them Hope about the Future

In an interview on Fox News Network, Miss Teen USA, 17-year-old Vanessa Minnillo, from Charleston, South Carolina, was asked by news analyst Bill O'Reilly what she thought about the Clinton scandal. She responded that she thought everyone has a personal and private life. When O'Reilly reminded her that the president was a role model, she replied that all of us are imperfect. He asked her how she thought young people in general were responding to the president's admission and she said that all the talk about impeachment was more a matter of concern for the older generation. She indicated that her generation was more interested in what they were wearing to the prom than what Clinton did. She did not feel that it was a major topic of conversation among teens.

Miss Teen USA is probably right. Teenagers value the instant. They don't have the experience of living for years and seeing the changes in society. They tend to live for the present and the short term. The same is true for children. Part of their outlook is tainted by the prevailing instant gratification attitude of our present society, but much of it is simply their age. They do not naturally think wisely about the future. They need us to interpret. Our teenagers and children can develop a respect for the future and for the past if we help them develop a healthy viewpoint as they grow.

Opportunities to Demonstrate Your Lifelong Commitment

When trauma or transition strikes a family, a neighborhood, a city, or a country, it causes feelings of chaos and confusion. That is true for us as adults and it is certainly true for our children. Whether it is a school shooting, cancer, going off to college, divorce, death, a move, or the actions of a president, we can assure our children that our commitment to them will not waver. We will remain faithful to them just as God will.

As authors Gary Smalley and John Trent wrote in *Home Remedies*, it's the kind of commitment that says, "You're important to me today and tomorrow, no matter what happens—no matter what the cost."[7] The authors make it a point to tell their children that they are committed to them for a lifetime, no matter what they do.

- *We are committed to help them be successful in whatever they want to do.*
- *We will be committed to them after they are married.*
- *We will be committed to them no matter whom they marry.*
- *We will be committed to them no matter what happens during their marriage.*
- *We will be committed to their mates and to their children.*
- *We will always be available to listen.*
- *Should they get into trouble, we will be there to help.*

Both men stress that these statements do not mean they will necessarily bail their kids out of a rough spot, because that may not be what is best in helping them ultimately to learn to be successful. But they want their children to know how much they love them.

When parents demonstrate God's faithfulness through their love and faithfulness to their children, they are putting "money" in the bank for their most precious lifelong investment.

Take the following Faithfulness Test. Talk and pray about the results.

The Faithfulness Test

Check your answers to the following questions.

1. How faithful are you to keep your promises to your children?

   ☐ Do it every time

   ☐ Trying hard

   ☐ Really struggling

   ☐ Blown it

2. How faithful are you to your job?

   ☐ 100 percent

   ☐ I'm there in body every day

   ☐ I call in sick a lot

   ☐ What job?

3. How faithful are you to your church?

   ☐ We open the doors

   ☐ We make sure the kids are there

   ☐ I don't sleep in worship

   ☐ We went on Easter Sunday

4. How faithful are you to being involved in the lives of your children?

   ☐ That is what my job is

   ☐ I coached Little League a couple of years ago

   ☐ I can't do everything

5. How faithful are you to being honest?

   ☐ I try to be honest in everything I do

   ☐ I only lie on my income tax

   ☐ Everyone lies sometimes

   Faithfulness is the beginning of honesty. How honest do you really want your child to be? The outcome depends on how faithful you are.

3
SELF-DISCIPLINE

"It hurts me more than it hurts you." Did your parents ever say that to you when you were disciplined? Whether you had to spend time alone in your room, miss a favorite TV show, or even endure a quick spanking, it was hard to see how this discipline was causing any pain to your parents. Nonetheless, the chances are great that your parents' firm and consistent discipline is what reinforced the value of self-discipline you have today.

The word *discipline* means "moral training." This word is different than the word *punish*. A parent's discipline should not *punish* the child for failing but rather focus on training for the future. Ironically, in order to effectively discipline a child, the parent must have *self*-discipline. To successfully implement any teaching or parenting strategy, parents must have the discipline of an athlete or musician. It requires discipline to develop clear expectations and to follow through with predictable and constant feedback. This means that the child is held accountable and responsible at every turn; the parents act firmly, gently, and predictably in praise and in discipline; and the parents model this lifestyle consistently.[8]

Getting in Control

Is your life out of control? Some people are extremely disciplined with work habits yet go on wild spending sprees and end up owing more than they make. Others are disciplined with their work and family yet are completely out of control with their eating habits, using food as a way of masking emotional distress. Still others are unable to control their sexual urges and act out on them even though they are committed to monogamous relationships. Sadly, when we lose self-control and act out on impulse, we not only hurt the very essence of our character—who we really are—but our loved ones suffer as well.

Having self-discipline is what separates us from animals. Whether from eating until they are ill or having many sexual encounters, animals cannot abstain. You can train an animal to show a certain amount of discipline, but the animal cannot make that decision himself. It is a uniquely human ability to have self-discipline and to control wants and desires.

Society challenges us to show our worldly strength by giving in to secular pleasures. But the challenge of Christians today is to follow Jesus no matter where society would have us go. It only takes looking at the lives of respected heroes and sheroes to know that discipline is a good thing. It first comes from recognizing our dependence on God and our need for His Spirit's changing power in our lives.

Think of where the world would be today without rules and discipline! Everyone would be doing whatever felt good, aiming for immediate gratification at the moment without any consideration of others or the consequences of their behavior.

Our world depends on rules and consequences to function. To raise an honest child, you must establish yourself as the "head" of the home—the one in charge. Then, balanced with lovingkindness, your firm and consistent discipline will enable your child to grow and develop into a responsible and honest adult.

What's important in teaching self-discipline? Here are some suggestions.

Build Self-Image

> *Having gifts that differ according to the grace given to us, let us use them: if prophecy, in proportion to our faith; if service, in our serving; he who teaches, in his teaching; he who exhorts, in his exhortation; he who contributes, in liberality; he who gives aid, with zeal; he who does acts of mercy, with cheerfulness.*
> *Romans 12:6–8 RSV*

M. Scott Peck, the popular psychiatrist who wrote *The Road Less Traveled*, connects a good self-image with self-discipline. Peck contends that the feeling of being valuable is the cornerstone of self-discipline. When we consider ourselves valuable we will take care of ourselves in all the ways necessary. "Self-discipline is self-caring."

A child cannot have good self-esteem without firm parental discipline. Dr. Diana Baumrind of the University of California at Berkeley has studied how various types of parental control affect children. She has found that the most assertive, self-reliant, and self-controlled children had parents who were "controlling, demanding, communicative, and loving." In the same study, children with the least self-reliance had parents who were loving but noncontrolling and nondemanding.[9] While love and kindness are important to boosting a child's self-image, equally important are firmness, rules, and regulations.

A parent builds a child's self-image by providing opportunities for success in life. This does not mean that every child must be the most successful child in the world's eyes. We can't all hit the winning home run, win the school spelling bee, or play a piano concerto. But each child can be encouraged to be all God has intended. Parents can nurture self-awareness and self-confidence by providing a variety of positive experiences—from sports teams to music and art lessons, to church music programs, to home projects, to quiet creative time—allowing the child to succeed at his level.

As you build self-esteem, it is important to acknowledge your child's gifts—yes, we all do have special gifts from God!—and teach him to lean on them, even when other parts of his life seem dismal.

A Personal Note

When Ashley was in fifth grade, she felt different than many of her classmates. Instead of being social and worrying about which boy she was going to go out with, she still enjoyed being a child—playing with her brother and sister, riding bikes, and spending evenings practicing piano. At that time, her peers were too self-absorbed in clothes and the opposite sex to affirm her gift of music, and she could not understand the need they had to grow up so fast. The more her peers pulled away, the more Ashley poured herself into playing piano, finding great reward in mastering difficult pieces. Eight years later, Ashley is an extremely self-confident and self-disciplined young adult and is double majoring in music and psychology at Emory University. She now looks back on her preteen years and is thankful she was able to find solace in her God-given talent when her goals and values differed from her peers.

Deb

As Christians, we make up a unique body of Christ with different interests, different talents, and different skills. But because God has created us all in His image as unique individuals, there is a niche for everyone. No two of us have the same fingerprints or footprints. Did you know that each of us even has our own tongue print? Yes, at the basic level of our existence, we are all unique, and this must be instilled in our children to strengthen their self-image.

Affirm Your Child's Strengths

> "Sons are a heritage from the LORD, children are a reward from Him." (Psalm 127:3)

Feeling good about ourselves is becoming rare, especially in a world where we are confronted with many daily situations that tear down our self-esteem. Yet if it is difficult for a mature adult to maintain a positive attitude and self-image, how much more difficult is it for a young, developing child to feel secure!

The Bible affirms the uniqueness of each child: "Then little children were brought to Jesus for Him to place His hands on them and pray for them. But the disciples rebuked those who brought them. Jesus said, 'Let the little children come to Me, and do not hinder them, for the kingdom of heaven belongs to such as these'" (Matthew 19:13–14).

What you say and how you act toward your child has a tremendous influence on his life and developing self-esteem. Your thoughts, feelings, and behavior mirror your soul. If you are full of negative thoughts, doubts, and suspicions regarding your child, then his attitude toward life becomes negative. But if you are enthusiastic, hopeful, and positive, your parenting skills can be filled with meaning. Your actions and words can have a vibrant impression on your children, especially as you raise them in the unique manner in which God intended.

What are your child's strengths and talents? Is he athletic or musical? Perhaps she is an excellent student or compassionate with friends. Talk with your child, and see what she feels her gifts are. Write down everything that comes to mind, as shown on the facing page, and post your list on the refrigerator to reinforce the behavior in your home.

Kim's Amazing Talents!

1. Kim is happy and has a positive attitude.

2. Kim is sincere and honest.

3. Kim is a good singer.

4. Kim is a good friend.

5. Kim got an A in math and science.

6. Kim enjoys gymnastics.

7. Kim helps with dinner.

8. Kim reads to her brother at night.

9. Kim sings in children's choir.

10. Kim is a Sunday school helper.

Talk about this list. Refer to it, and affirm the child's talents and gifts every morning before your breakfast prayer, thanking God for your child's special gifts. As you build on your child's talents and gifts, you help her to accept areas in her life that she may have no control over. Isn't that a strength in itself—to accept our weaknesses? Personal weaknesses that used to haunt your child will diminish—if you continue to affirm her and focus on her developing self-image.

Love Your Child—No Strings Attached

"If only he were a better student."

"She is a good reader but so poor in math."

The problem with constantly worrying that your child is not performing perfectly is that you often fail to love the child at that moment for who he is—no strings attached. Instead, you love him for how he looks, what he achieves, or how well he sings, dances, or does cartwheels in gymnastics.

Because of Christ, God accepts us right where we are in life—warts and all. God loves us even though we have faults, even though we are weak, even though we cannot sing, dance, or do cartwheels! God's love is so amazing that it's there for us when we lose our jobs, lose our friends, or even lose our spouse to divorce. We are loved with no strings attached ... simply because.

To be accepting in our families, we must imitate this all-powerful and unconditional love Jesus taught. Embrace your child each day, whether you feel like it or not, and accept him on the spot. It is only when we become accepting of others—faults and all—that we can begin to help them grow.

How do you get to know your child better? Try these 10 ways:

1. Turn off the television.

2. Have family meals.

3. Talk with your child one-to-one.

4. Play a board game.

5. Work (or play) on the computer—together.

6. Teach your child a skill or hobby.

7. Watch his favorite TV show with him and talk about it.

8. Talk to her about things that happened when you were her age.

9. Pray aloud together.

10. Teach his Sunday school class.

Encourage Independence

Part of raising a self-disciplined child is teaching him to be independent. This means never doing anything for the child that he can do for himself. For busy parents, this rule is difficult, especially when mornings are hurried and harried trying to make car pools and get to work. But the child who is able to choose his clothes, dress himself, organize his room, and take care of school homework— without parental intervention—is the child who will have an easier time in life.

"But he hates putting his own shoes on, so I dress him to avoid conflict before school." How many parents have said that before! Keep in mind that small whiners grow up to be tall complainers as they have developed no "struggle muscle." They constantly search for friends and spouses who will take care of them just like Mom did. These frustrated people never struggled with who they were or who they would become because that was hard work, and as you may have experienced, Mom or Dad did all the work.

Raising self-disciplined children mandates that parents back off, and let the child become responsible for his own actions—and consequences—as we break the "helicopter parent" pattern. (This is the parent who constantly hovers over her young just waiting to rescue them from failure or frustration.) If you make your child's world too "perfect," how will he cope in the real world? Not very easily!

If you can think back to your own childhood, you will realize that it was those frustrations, setbacks, and even disappointments that helped you figure out what it took to be more independent. That's how we learn to cope, regroup, and try again when life gets tough. And as you may have experienced, life will get tough! So, what's the answer? Expect more from your child—not less. If your child is not helping out at home, give him more responsibilities. Keep in mind that a child who can log on to the Internet to find his favorite website can certainly fold a basket of laundry. Let him be a real-world participant in your family and reap the strength of having self-discipline.

Affirm Assertiveness

It's important to distinguish between "assertiveness" and "aggressiveness." Assertiveness means your child can stick up for herself instead of following the ways of the crowd. A child who is assertive is usually very confident, positive, and affirming. On the other hand, an aggressive child is one who is often negative and hostile.

Give your child situations where she has to stand up for what she believes. You might ask her to tell why she enjoys a favorite author or television show. Try to argue her points to see if she can hold her own in standing up for what she likes. Explain that sometimes in life people will challenge her values, and she must continue to stand confident and affirm what she knows to be right.

Stand Strong

Train a child in the way he should go, and
when he is old he will not turn from it.
Proverbs 22:6

The word *authority* often has negative connotations for some well-meaning parents, yet in Ephesians 6:1–2 we find, "Children, obey your parents; this is the right thing to do because God has placed them in authority over you. Honor your father and mother" (TLB). This passage gives the ultimate standard for the behavior of a child with obedience and respect being vital attributes. But the Scripture also gives a forthright directive for parents—to be authoritative or the expert in the family—"because God has placed them in authority over you."

For the Christian family, being authoritative means being loving and responsible. Parents convey trust and confidence to their children when they take the role of authority, thus giving security and strength to the family unit.

> *Several recently completed studies that tracked more than 100 children for nearly 20 years have provided the first objective test of which disciplinary styles work best, and all point in the same direction. Parents who are not harshly punitive, but who set firm boundaries and stick to them, are significantly more likely to produce children who are high achievers and get along well with others.*

Define Your Parenting Style

Type	Definition
Authoritarian	Do it because I'm your parent.
Authoritative	Do it for this reason.
Permissive	Do whatever you want.

A set of longitudinal studies at the University of California at Berkeley's Institute of Human Development affirms the need to be authoritative. Researchers disclosed that "Authoritarian" parents were more likely to have discontented children. "Permissive" parents had children who were the least self-reliant and curious about the world, and who took the fewest risks. "Authoritative" parents were more likely to have self-reliant, self-controlled, contented children. For Christian parents, of course, the "reason" we point to is both "This is what God says in His commandments" and "Because Jesus so loved us we want to grow as God's children."

Sometimes we cannot honestly explain why a child must or must not do something. You might have to rely on an internal "gut" instinct as you issue rules and limitations. Remember, it is far better to be authoritative and risk seeming unfair at times, than to risk raising children who do not respect adults or rules.

Let Your Discipline Fit the Incident

> *And now a word to you parents. Don't keep on*
> *scolding and nagging your children, making*
> *them angry and resentful. Rather, bring them up*
> *with the loving discipline the Lord Himself*
> *approves, with suggestions and godly advice.*
> Ephesians 6:4 TLB

Parenting is about relationships—loving relationships. To discipline your child effectively, spend time with him and get to know him. If your parent-child relationship is devoted and respectful, your discipline will be more tolerated than if a child resents you as a dictator. When rules are broken, make sure the discipline you administer is firm but kind. You may consider these questions:

- *Does the discipline method fit the incident?*
- *Was the discipline method given in a fit of anger or was it well thought-out?*
- *Is the discipline method age-appropriate?*
- *Will you follow through with the discipline or let it go?*
- *Can the child grow through the discipline choice and learn from his or her mistakes?*

Parents can be authoritative and firm disciplinarians in the home without striking a child, and this does not mean you are "sparing the rod." To "spare the rod" means not to discipline the child. Taking away worldly pleasures such as television, radio, video games, telephones, or playing with friends is probably more likely to get a child's attention and call for behavioral changes than hitting him. And when you use reasonable consequences, you never have to live with that horrible fear of physically hurting your child when you lose control. Stick to non-physical methods of discipline—they do work!

Discipline in the family is not about being mean to a child, nor is it about making life miserable for the parents—and it can! Discipline is about

- *Teaching children to follow well-established rules*
- *Teaching children to stay within given limits*
- *Teaching children that when rules are broken, there are consequences to pay*

The Strong-Willed or Spirited Child

A Personal Note

I will admit that I was a strong-willed or spirited child. Now it wasn't that I was a bad child (of course, this is my opinion!), but I had all the innate, irritating qualities that could trigger hostility in the most patient parent. Interestingly, my negative childhood qualities of being inflexible, unwavering, stubborn, and unyielding became positive adult strengths as friends tell me I am determined, persistent, faithful, and persevering. Don't give up on your strong-willed child. Find what works and use it!

Deb

If you have a strong-willed or spirited child, you know it is often a winless situation to use traditional discipline methods, especially on days when you "lock horns" and no one will budge. But there are some innovative changes you can make in your discipline style that may help to channel your child's willfulness without breaking his precious spirit.

1. **Call a cease fire.** Before you can help to channel your child's determination, it is important to understand your own personality:

   - *Are you just as persistent as your child?*

   - *Is winning always important to you?*

   - *Or can you sometimes let minor issues slide while focusing on what is really important in your child's life?*

   Many strong-willed children have parents who are just as stubborn and forceful. This sets the stage for a perpetual battlefield in the home if you don't recognize the problem and make plans to change. While controlling your child's behavior 100 percent of the time is impossible, you can make changes in your parenting behavior, including how you act and react to what he says or does.

2. **Watch your reaction.** Strong-willed children love to watch their parents' reactions to their stubborn ways. You ask your spirited child to hurry and get dressed, and he leisurely crosses his arms across his chest, sticks out his bottom lip and says, "Nope. I don't want to." How do you react? If you are like most parents, your first reaction is to raise your voice in anger, then show your rage with seething facial gestures.

To teach self-discipline, *you* must have self-discipline! Do not give your child the pleasure of seeing you angry because of his behavior. Children will demand your attention—positive or negative. Knowing this, make sure the attention you give your child is positive. React positively to his obedient behaviors and deal with his negative behaviors in a mature, disciplined way—no wrath, no fury, and no out-of-control rampage.

3. **Remember the moment.** Now you are wondering, how will my child know I am upset if I do not yell or show it? Don't avoid showing anger. Rather, pick the *right* moment. When your children are in stubborn stages, you can stay angry 24 hours a day if you react to each of their whims. There are better ways to react than anger, especially with a determined child who is insensitive to most forms of discipline.

   With an older preschooler or elementary-age child, tell her up front that you will "remember any moment" that she does not obey you. How is this put into practice? If your child enjoys making crafts with markers, glue, and trails of paper, and refuses to clean up after enjoying this activity, quietly say to her, "I will remember this moment." She may look at you puzzled and wonder why you aren't nagging, yelling, or threatening with another timeout. But the next day when she is bored to tears and wants to pull out the craft supplies, smile and refuse to get the supplies down. Reaffirm that you remember how she was irresponsible the day before, and she must wait until tomorrow to do crafts. Yes, you remembered her negative moment, and gave her time to rethink her actions. This type of natural consequence works when you ask your child to clean off the table, pick up her bicycle, or even get dressed for school. No anger is shown, and it works like a charm!

4. **Work it out.** If timeout is pleasing to your strong-willed child, change your method to a punishment that fits the "crime." Let your child do a chore for his punishment. This could be sweeping the kitchen floor several times during the day, washing the sliding glass doors, or weeding a garden. A younger child may wipe off cabinets with a damp cloth or pick up toys.

   Active punishment enables your child to think about his "crime" and also lets him accomplish something necessary for living together as a family. Reinforce this important value of everyone pitching in and getting along in your family as you follow through with the consequence.

5. **Lean on humor.** Yes, raising strong-willed or spirited children is quite a challenge, but sometimes you have to lighten up!

Self-discipline is a vital value for parents to
live and teach, but when the standard methods don't work, you have to search for alternatives. And who said that discipline has to
be harsh? Especially for strong-willed or
spirited children who often thrive on defying
authority, find the type of discipline that
works for your child. Make it fit the incident,
and use it consistently to make him mind …
without losing yours.

Create Family Rituals

In our transient, fast-paced society where family
time is often diluted, rituals are vital. They offer a sense of
identity in an impersonal era; they bond the family members to one another and help us to become rooted in the
world. And it is these roots that will strengthen our children when we are faced with problems in life.

According to Tony Campolo, an American Baptist
clergyman and teacher at Eastern College in St. Davids,
Pennsylvania, rituals provide a sense of solidarity or
belonging, enhanced loyalty, education from generation
to generation, and emotional stability in the family.

Speaking at a national United Methodist Conference
called "Family '98," Campolo infused his message with
examples of religious groups that have achieved oneness
through rituals. The key to solidarity among Roman
Catholics, he said, has been the mass which had been performed uniformly by Catholics all over the world. When
the tradition of the mass changed (no longer using Latin),
solidarity in the church began to fall apart. Campolo con-

tends that even opening Christmas gifts can be a meaningful process in the family that helps us to recreate the past and regenerate what has been lost.

You can start new rituals for your family. This could be waking up a bit earlier to have breakfast together or spending time after dinner playing a board game or musical instruments. You might make one night "Family Night," when just your immediate family members spend time together, go to a movie, out to dinner, or watch a video.

Rituals strengthen the structure in the family, especially if it is something you can look forward to on a regular basis. Rituals will help increase your trust in one another as you know that in the midst of a harried life, there are some things you can still count on to be the same.

Family traditions are also ageless. They bridge us with our past in a manner that offers comfort and reassurance. When an aging grandparent comments to the young teen, "This tiny angel on your tree was mine when I was a young girl," all generations feel a warm sense of connectedness. In simpler terms, family traditions make us feel loved.

What are some family traditions you can pass on to your children?

- *Identify a favorite family recipe.* When you make that favorite chicken-rice casserole, change the ingredients enough to make it yours. Using your family's name, claim this as your traditional recipe (such as the Smith Family Chicken Casserole or Grandma's Chicken Surprise).

- *Plant a tree together.* Go as a family to pick out the tree. Celebrate afterwards as your family pitches *dirt around the tree and makes its mark in the neighborhood.*

- **Share lasting memories.** *Look through old family albums and talk about your childhood.*
- **Eat out after church on Sunday.** *Call it your special family luncheon. Make this something your children look forward to and expect to happen each week.*
- **Celebrate special moments in childhood.** *The first day of school, a pulled tooth, learning to ride a bike or even drive a car—these are all momentous times in a family's life. Let your family know that these are times when you all join together to affirm the accomplishment.*

What about Manners?

It's probably no news to you that children are not born knowing manners; it is an important discipline that must be taught to have a self-disciplined child.

Values Check

I Lead, You Follow

Teaching manners means teaching a child to live within the rules—the rules of behavior toward others. You teach manners by explanation and example, and the key word your child should learn is respect—respect for all people.

Be an excellent role model. Watch what you do because they watch what you do! Be a mannerly role model. Teach your child to do the following.

- *Say "please" and "thank you."*
- *Say "excuse me" when he gets up from the table.*

- *Not speak when someone else is talking at the table or in a group.*
- *Use silverware—not fingers—when eating, and put her napkin on her lap.*
- *Look adults in the eye when speaking.*
- *Use a whisper in church.*
- *Use responsible telephone manners.*
- *Respect your privacy when you are on the telephone.*

You and I Lead Together
- *Use role play for young children. Spend time "pretending" as you offer your child a gift and he politely says "thank you." In your most gracious voice say "thank you" as your child pretends to give you a gift.*
- *Encourage him to say "please" and "thank you" as you offer a glass of juice, and remind him gently when he forgets.*
- *Using her tiniest tea set, play "tea party" in the dining room and show her how to sit up straight, put her napkin in her lap, ask politely for the cookies to be passed, and excuse herself when she is through.*

You Lead, I Follow

When your child forgets his manners—and he will—kindly state the rules of etiquette repeatedly, in a positive voice, until your child picks up on them and repeats them herself.

Older Children and Teens

If your teen is out of control and lacking in self-discipline, obviously you cannot turn back the clock and recapture what is past. But you can begin today—right now—to raise your child in a disciplined family using common sense to guide your actions as you lean on biblical premises.

Hug Even When Unhuggable

Learn to value the healing power of touch when a teen is in an unlovely stage. This power seems to melt even the most bitter moment and usually is the security the adolescent longs for. While our society has been conditioned to be hands-off, touch may be that special key to an on-going positive self-esteem. A pat on the shoulder after a firm reprimand, a loving hug after unlovely moments, or a caring back rub after a family upset are often just as appreciated as saying the words "I care."

Respect Even When Disrespectful

Teenagers, especially difficult ones, learn to respect other adults as they are shown respect by their parents. When raising a difficult teen, try to avoid speaking down to her, even if you are reprimanding her. Often it is helpful to ask, "Would I say that to a friend?" before speaking. As you carefully adjust your tone of voice, the teen will react with more respect. You might find that some discipline problems can be cured by talking through negative situations and letting the teenager have a say in making family rules.

Lean on Biblical Virtues

There are many virtues the Bible describes when it comes to living the full Christian life. These virtues are to be used enthusiastically, especially when difficult teenagers tempt your patience.

- *Have patience.* The challenge of Hebrews 12:1 is this: "Let us run with perseverance the race marked out for us." This patience involves not giving up in times of crisis, but "hanging in" and accepting the situation until changes occur.

- *Be persistent.* Luke offers more strength for being steadfast in Acts 2:42, "They devoted themselves to the apostles' teaching and to the fellowship, to the breaking of bread and to prayer." Persistence involves loyalty to the young person's potential instead of what you might see at a bad moment—yes, sometimes you must look for the good qualities. In trying moments, take a time out to your bedroom, and use your head and heart as you relate to your teen on a level that believes in and encourages his strengths and attributes.

- *Be in prayer.* The psalmist says, "Evening, morning and noon I cry out in distress, and He hears my voice" (Psalm 55:17). God hears our prayers. If there is a broken relationship in your family, pray, asking God to unite the members. Prayer is a special communication that enables the difficult teen to know of God's love and power, even when the enthusiasm is not felt. And prayer can be the serenity a distraught parent needs during moments of anguish.

- *See the possibility.* In Mark 14:36, Jesus prayed, "Abba, Father ... everything is possible for You. Take this cup from Me. Yet not what I will, but what You will." Paul teaches in Philippians 4:13, "I can do everything through Him who gives me strength." Our Christian faith is one of trusting that Jesus has the power through the Spirit to change even the most difficult teenager.

Teaching self-discipline means you will spend a great deal of time and energy being explicit about your family's rules, consistent in how you follow up on rule-breakers, and firm but kind with disciplinary actions. It means setting limits and giving consequences even when you are tired or busy or distracted.

Learn from the Past

It's not easy raising kids. Our own myriad parenting mistakes could be written as a thick sequel to this book. In fact, strong parents make as many and as ghastly mistakes as weak parents. Nonetheless, you can learn from your past and avoid making the same mistakes again.

Remember, even when your parenting mistakes seem numerous, you can cling to the grace and forgiveness of God. Grace is how God deals with us far beyond what we deserve; His forgiveness is the cooling salve which heals the gaping wounds of guilt and shame so many parents carry with them. Ask God to guide your family as you regroup and focus on self-discipline.

④
ACCOUNTABILITY

No one likes to be wrong. The list of excuses our children give when faced with a wrongdoing can be overwhelming:

"I didn't do it, I promise."

"If the teacher liked me, I wouldn't have failed that test."

"It's your fault, not mine. You should have looked to make sure my bike wasn't behind the car before you ran over it."

"If the teacher had quizzed us on the right material, I would have passed."

"If Dad had put a better lock on the door, the dog wouldn't have slipped out."

"I wouldn't have hit him, but he looked like he was ready to hit me."

"I would have made curfew if the clock at the movie theater was accurate."

And the list goes on with either a prefabricated excuse for an irresponsible wrongdoing or a scapegoat to blame for their failure. As parents, we've heard it all. Nonetheless, we know that if our children are to be held accountable for their actions and words, we must lead the way by modeling a Christlike lifestyle.

It's Not My Fault

History is full of examples that lend credence to the idea that blaming others can benefit us. Yet in a society that seems to thrive on litigation and accusations, just how can a parent teach children to be accountable for their actions?

Dr. Eric Dlugokinski, psychologist and professor, speaks to the problem of blaming others for our own mistakes, saying that transcending the "psychology of victimization" requires determination, commitment, and a recognition of reality because if life is like a box of chocolates as Forrest Gump says, then blame is like a boomerang.

"The more you blame, the more blame comes back to you," Dlugokinski says. "If you don't know where your responsibilities start and stop, you continue blaming others and stay in an emotional rut forever."[10]

Blaming others for our misfortunes is a primitive mindset that goes back to childhood. As children, some of us believed it was our mother's fault that we had to get out of bed in the morning and go to school. We may have grown up believing that everyone else is responsible for our discomfort and, as adults, we still may believe that.

Discomfort is a part of living. We assume responsibility for our own lives at some point, and we need to learn to cope with difficulties in daily living.

A Personal Assessment

Several years ago, a Florida couple made nationwide headlines. They earned this publicity by instructing their teenagers on the ins and outs of the "family business." It just so happened that the family business was armed robbery. This mother and father were thoroughly schooling their teenage sons in such tools of the trade as AK-47 assault rifles, police scanners, escape routes, surveillance and survival gear, and disguises. They carefully taught them hand-to-hand combat and expected their sons to memorize police codes and map layouts. After each robbery, the boys were debriefed and their mistakes were discussed and corrected.

The sad part of this story is that for the most part, these parents were far more serious about training their sons for armed robbery than many Christian parents are about teaching children personal responsibility. How can we teach responsibility at home? By being accountable for our behaviors in how we handle relationships with

- *God through Jesus Christ*
- *Our spouse*
- *Our children*
- *Our friends, coworkers, neighbors, acquaintances, and even enemies*
- *The "least of these"—the weak, sick, lonely, and others in need*

In other words, we are accountable for taking personal responsibility in all we do—the good and bad—as we strive to live a Christlike life. In fact, what you say and how you act and react in your home right now gives your child internal guidelines that will govern her actions in years to come. If you are acting irresponsibly at home, why should your child demonstrate any different behavior? If you are irritable, easy to anger, and fail to take responsibility for negative behaviors, you are raising a child who is destined to follow this path. And if you fail to pray, ask for God's guidance in your home, or read the Bible for a greater understanding of the faith, your child will mimic the same.

You Are the Best Christian Someone Else Knows

Think of all the people across the globe who have never seen a Bible, never heard the Scriptures read. But they see us. They hear us. Are those around you "seeing God" in your words, your actions, and your reactions in life? Do others say about you: "He or she reminds me of Jesus"? Does your light so shine that it touches those around you? Let your life and light reflect your salvation in Jesus Christ.

> *[Jesus said,] "By this all men will know that you*
> *are My disciples, if you love one another."*
> *John 13:35*

Making Memories that Last

What will your child remember about her home life? Will she remember the arguments at bedtime; the sulking stares across the dinner table; the fights over who is spending too much money? Or will she cherish memories filled with the warmth, compassion, and affection you have for your family members?

Before you respond, it is important to understand the two levels of memory. There is the surface level: the memory of the climbing tree where you spent hours as a child; the memory of the sweet perfume your mother wore; the memory of your father's hands worn rough by years of labor.

These are important memories, but there is another level of memory: that deep inner reservoir of memory called the subconscious. From our subconscious comes our motivation and actions, which come out of our values.

The writer of Proverbs spoke about the power of the subconscious: "Keep your heart with all vigilance; for from it flow the springs of life" (Proverbs 4:23 RSV). Luke 6:45 records that Jesus said it is out of the heart that come those things which either make or destroy a person.

These two biblical writers suggest that the subconscious has no digestive tract. In other words, be careful what you feed into your child's memory because it might become the motivating force of his life!

Teach Them Well

"If this is true, our child's future is already doomed," you might say. Let's be honest: we all make mistakes in life; no one is innocent of this. We all admit to having experienced "off" moments when one of us is irritable or loses his temper. Who hasn't been rude to a telephone solicitor during the dinner hour? What about neighbor-love? We each recall times when we grumbled about the neighbor's child in our yard or the tree shedding leaves on our property. Nonetheless, if your relationships with others have been filled with more negatives than positives, it is never too late to ask God for forgiveness. Ask Him to change your attitude and how you deal with others. This forgiveness frees us to make changes in our lives—both separately and together.

Model Responsibility

Observe your behavior. Step back today and see how your child perceives your actions and words. Listen to how you talk to your spouse, a friend on the telephone, the repairman, and your neighbor. What is your tone of voice? Is it loving or apathetic? Watch how you act and react to what these people say to you. Do you listen and really hear what the other person is saying? Is your tone of voice kind and empathetic or harsh and short? Use this process of observation to make much-needed changes in the way you relate to people.

Remember that love is more than a feeling. Convey to your child through actions and words that loving others goes beyond feelings, that you can love and respect each person for being a child of God—especially when you don't feel like it. This take-away value will enable your children to stand strong during life's ebbs and flows. You can

- *Give your spouse or child a kiss on the cheek when he is tired and cranky.*
- *Pray for your employer or coworkers when job stresses surmount.*

- *Count to 10 before saying unkind words during a disagreement with your spouse, child, neighbor, or friend.*
- *Call someone you've disagreed with and work to build bridges in your relationship.*

Let your children see you really care about others as you work at making life better for family and friends, leaning on the little things in life to strengthen the whole. This take-away value will serve as a gentle daily reminder for your children of the true meaning of Christlike love. You can

- *Call your spouse before leaving work to see if anything is needed from the store.*
- *Iron a blouse for your teenager when she is late for school.*
- *Offer to do chores or cook for a new mother in your neighborhood.*
- *Send your pastor and Sunday school teachers a supportive note, and let your child sign it with you.*
- *Write an apology note to a friend expressing your desire to forgive and make amends.*

Love and respect all God's children. Teach your child that it matters to you what kind of world you pass on to her. This take-away value will give your child strength of character and compassion in her life as she works to make a difference at home and in the world. You can

- *Work in the church, teaching a class or singing in the choir.*
- *Volunteer to lead a committee at your child's school.*
- *Offer to tutor children with disabilities.*
- *Adopt a family and provide holiday meals and gifts.*

Love and serve God. Let your children know that the Christian life is more than just a Sunday morning experience; it is a joyous celebration of your entire life. This take-away value can allow your children to someday say to their mates, "Being a Christian was the most exciting thing I ever saw Mom and Dad do!" You can

- *Join hands and pray together each night.*
- *Read the Bible aloud to your children.*
- *Worship as a family.*
- *Talk openly about your relationship with Jesus Christ and how He helps you to love others in your family, neighborhood, school, work, etc.*

Watch What You Do ...
Because They Watch What You Do!

When he is an adult, what memories will your child have of you being responsible for his life? Will your child remember that you loved and cared for others, that Christ was at the helm of your home? Or will he remember your home as a constant battleground, a place for fighting, winning, losing, and keeping score?

The good news is that our past is just that—the past. Leaning on the grace of God, make plans to rewrite your "script," changing negative behaviors, focusing on positive actions, and affirming the Christlike love you hold on to. Once you've started on the path to being responsible in all areas of life, you can expect the same from your child. Hold your child accountable for every action—and reaction—he takes.

Right or Wrong—It's Your Choice

Parents are responsible not only for what we say and how we treat others, but also for teaching our children to be accountable for their actions. Children need to know how to make wise decisions—and the consequences they will suffer when they don't. Remember when making decisions was as easy as saying, "One potato, two potato, three potato, four …"? Maybe you picked flower petals saying, "He loves me, he loves me not …" While these methods are fun, making responsible decisions is not a random procedure.

Values Check

I Lead, You Follow

- *Let your child see how God's love and compassion influences what you eat, drink, watch on television, read, or even the people you associate with. Your lifestyle habits will set a precedent for his when he grows up.*
- *Talk about making good decisions. Tell your child why you chose a certain television show or video. With conversation, you can help her learn to see both pros and cons of making a decision.*

You and I Lead Together

Offer choices. Depending on the child's maturity, start with simple choices that affect his daily life. For example, "Do you want peanut butter or cheese on your sandwich?" or "Do you want to wear your sweater or sweatshirt today?"

As the child learns to make a reasonable choice and live with the result, you can add more complex choices, asking: "Do you want to buy the hot lunch, buy a sandwich, or take your lunch box today?" or "Do you want to invite Sammy over today, work on your new clubhouse, or play your video game?"

You Lead, I Follow

Teach your child to consider the alternatives. Each time he makes a choice, talk about the alternatives by asking: "Why did you choose that?" or "Is there another choice that would also work?"

Discuss the consequences. Every action your child takes has a reaction, either good or bad. Help your child think through the pros and cons of his choices by questioning:

1. How will that help you? Hurt you?

2. Is it respectful to all, including family and friends?

3. Will it hurt anyone else?

4. Do you feel comfortable with this decision?

5. What would Jesus do in this situation?

Evaluate the decision. Through evaluation your child can grow in wisdom in making more life choices even when his choices don't work out. Ask

1. Would you make the same choice next time? Why? Why not?

2. What would you do the same? Differently?

3. What did you learn from this?

Jesus' ministry was one of making choices. As He confronted people in different situations, He encouraged them to make firm commitments and decisions about their lives—to choose between good and evil. A uniqueness of the New Testament lies in this new freedom that Jesus taught, breaking us away from the bondage of Old Testament ceremonial laws.

As Christians, God calls us to be obedient in the midst of having freedom. By taking action and making solid life choices, we will model responsibility to our developing children.

Creative Problem Solving

Use the following outline to teach your child creative problem solving. Present a problem, then let him brainstorm all possible alternatives (even silly ones!). Discuss responsible decision making and making wise choices.

1. Present the problem.

2. Discuss the alternatives. (What other options are there?)

3. Think about the consequences. (List pros and cons of each.)

4. Evaluate the choice made. (Did it work? Why? Why not?)

Garbage In, Garbage Out

"Sticks and stones can break my bones, but words will never hurt me." Remember saying that as a young child when a friend assaulted you with offensive names? Being called a name by a sibling or peer does hurt. While name-calling is a normal behavior, it is also unacceptable. Hold your child accountable.

Teaching Accountability for Words

If your child is "guilty as charged," consider reasons he is using these words. Putting other people down or talking big can make a shy or hesitant child feel powerful and more accepted by the peers he is trying to impress. Some children may not have been taught at home that name-calling is unacceptable behavior. And other children may call their peers names because it gets attention—from other students as well as the teacher. For some kids, even negative attention is better than no attention at all.

Have firm family rules and appropriate limits. Tell your child sternly, "In our home we don't treat people that way. This is unacceptable behavior." If name-calling is not allowed in your home, make certain older siblings and adults abide by the rule.

Issue the consequences. Let your child know what will happen if you hear name-calling. For example, "If I hear you calling someone a name again, I will put you in your room (or time out)." Be sure to follow up consistently with the consequences should your child test his limits.

Teach empathy. Empathy helps your child feel what others are experiencing. Ask your child how he would feel if someone called him a name. Role play a situation where your child is the underdog and is being called names, then talk about the feelings he may have.

Reward positive behavior. As you see your child interact with peers, liberally compliment any positive behavior he exhibits. When he plays fairly, praise him. When he is kind and speaks kindly, let him know this pleases you too.

For most children, name-calling is a phase they will outgrow quickly. But to ensure your child's positive development, take steps ahead of time to teach your family's rules and the consequences should he break them. Keeping him accountable for his words and behaviors at a young age will help him become a responsible adult in years to come.

Where Do You Go When It Hurts?

Taking personal responsibility for life's disappointments or failures is another way your child can be accountable.

A Personal Note

Disappointment or feelings of failure can occur when a friend makes a promise to your child and doesn't keep it. When Brittnye's best friend invited her to spend a week at the beach with her family, she was thrilled. Yet when the time came for the long-awaited trip, a childish spat caused friction in their friendship, and the young friend invited someone else instead.

Deb

Often when children face failure or disappointment they begin to feel as if the world is against them. Some children develop a chip on their shoulders as they become engulfed in this defeated attitude. Apathy may begin to spread throughout the family, and the general attitude of all members can become negative. Usually more disappointments will occur as children halfheartedly attempt their goals in life.

You can help your child take personal responsibility for his failures—just as he does for any successes. By demonstrating your faith in the living God—a faith that calls for hope during times of trial—you can suggest ways of dealing positively with various disappointments.

Teaching Accountability for Defeat

Use the following questions to help your child grow and stop blaming the world for life's interruptions and defeats.

1. **Can the child talk openly about disappointments?** Bottled-up negative feelings only continue to grow. Yet when aired openly, these feelings can soon become a part of the past. Talking about failures or disappointments in the Christian home helps to ease the tension and anxiety. As children share their feelings of resentment and anger, the letdown seems to lessen in intensity.

2. **How can she find God amidst failure or disappointment?** There has been a life-

long debate on how to discern God's will for our lives. Yet, as Christians, we know that through listening to God, prayer, and Bible study, we can search for God's plan for us. Often as one door closes, bringing feelings of despair, other doors open leading to new and creative possibilities in life.

3. **Can she use the strength the Lord gives to move on in her life?** Major disappointments bring anguish in life. Children can sometimes feel that their world has fallen in. Yet God gives strength to begin anew. Fellowship and communication within the family are vital so strength can come from within this tightly knit unit.

4. **Can he forgive those who disappoint him?** The whole essence of the Gospel message lies in loving and forgiving. Yet as we harbor feelings of anguish after disappointing situations, forgiveness is unthought of. By placing our faith in God, by building our lives around His Word, through continual prayer, fellowship, and service, we can experience the strength to forgive those who hurt or disappoint us. Accepting others where they are instead of molding them into persons we want them to be helps to eliminate frustration and disappointments.

Accountability for Teens

Growing up begins earlier than ever before in our nation. Twenty years ago, a 4-year-old used to spend the day riding a tricycle; today she plays with her shapely fashion doll and the miniature sports car. A 9-year-old used to play hopscotch or kick ball with the neighborhood gang; now she giggles with her friends on her personal phone about the latest video on MTV. And a 12-year-old who used to innocently enter the teen years, speaks with pseudo-maturity about the facts of AIDS, sexually transmitted diseases, and homosexuality. Have we robbed our children of their childhood?

On Sex

Twenty years ago, parents took pride in protecting children from growing up too fast, holding them back from conversations and suggestions that were too "adult." We remember our own parents saying, "We don't discuss that in our family." But today's parents are forced to protect children from the perils of a fast-paced, hurried society with weakened morals and values. And sex is a mandatory discussion in most homes—not to encourage children to become active, but to alert them of the many hazards life has in store ... if they break the rules.

Spend time together. Continue to develop your parent-child relationship as your teen moves into older adolescence, making plans to be together without distractions like the television or phone. Go on long walks, go shopping, play golf, or go fishing—whatever you and your teen enjoy doing. This gives security to the teen—a positive weapon against peer pressure.

Have age-appropriate discussions. Most children, by the time they reach teenage years, have a great understanding of sexuality, but where did they learn it—from a friend, MTV, the latest teen magazine? Do they understand the Christian perspective? A 12-year-old boy may suddenly become enthralled with the bathing suit photographs in a sports magazine; a 14-year-old girl may bring home teen magazines with articles on flirting, dating, and sexual relationships. But reading secular articles on sex and dating or looking at an advertiser's portrayal of love does not let our teens know what we believe. By the age of 12, children should know the facts about sex and how it will affect them as they go through puberty. But also by this age, children should know from their parents the facts about the family's values—God's design for our sexuality as His good gift that is to be used responsibly.

Talk about right and wrong. Begin discussions about sex and the Christian perspective at an early age. Include a constant exchange of ideas. When children are in elementary school, they ask questions about sexual behavior. Answer the questions honestly, but also interject statements such as, "In our home, we feel that is wrong," or "As Christians, we know that sex is to be saved for marriage." If your children look at sexually candid billboards or television commercials, speak openly about what they are seeing and add your personal beliefs and testimony from God's Word. Rather than giving a negative impression about sexuality, affirm the beauty of sex as having God's blessings in the context of marriage.

Talk openly with your teen about sexual feelings and emphasize your Christian beliefs about abstinence until marriage. Let your older teen know what he will be faced with when he begins dating, and help him work through personal values, finding ways of saying no to aggressive dates. Talk with your older teen about how to treat a date with respect and courtesy.

Teach self-control, not birth control. When you talk with your teen about sex, emphasize self-control. Let your teen know that she is in charge of her body. You may want to introduce the following in your home:

1. God planned for sex within the context of marriage. He expects us to save sex for marriage and not to participate in lustful behavior (see Scripture Strengths below).

2. We (Mom and Dad) have the highest dreams for you. We want you to go to college, learn a trade, fulfill your goals, and use your talents. We want the best for you and want you to avoid the harmful consequences of premarital sex.

3. The cost of sex before marriage is high. From AIDS to sexually transmitted diseases to pregnancy—these don't have to be concerns for you if you say no to premarital sex.

Scripture Strengths
- *God created sex! Read Genesis 2:18–22 and Psalm 139:13.*
- *God has a plan for sex. Read Matthew 19:4–6 and Genesis 2:24.*

- *God gives instructions on sexuality.*
  Read Hebrews 13:14 and Galatians 3:19–20.

- *God has two reasons to wait.*
  Read Deuteronomy 10:12–13 and Jeremiah 29:11.

On Music

To many teens, music is their world. Although the music industry provides such great Christian artists as Point of Grace, Michael W. Smith, and 4 Him, many teens are still attracted to music filled with profanity, perverted thoughts, and suggestions of alternative lifestyles. Much of today's rap music places women in an inferior role, and if you listen carefully, some of the most popular rock groups speak favorably of drugs, alcohol, sexual involvement, and even suicide. Where do parents draw the line?

Although it is not mandatory in the record industry, music that may have questionable lyrics is usually marked with the label "Parental Advisory—Explicit Lyrics." While children and teens are still allowed to purchase this music, it does serve as a red flag for the parent. One national music and video chain takes this one step further and labels music that is inappropriate for teens with "Must be 18 or older to buy this item. ID required."

Go with your child to make these purchases. Ask the sales people to guide you as your child or teen makes selections, and use discretion—if you are not sure of a CD or tape's content, do not purchase it until you are. While it is difficult to give absolutes to older teens when they control the radio stations and tape or CD players in their cars, you will need to trust that your teen will make sound judgments while away from home. Continue talking about your family's values.

While it is normal for older teens to feel independent and to question the values they grew up with, if the platform of faith is strong, they will always have these values to fall back on. One method of getting teens to think about the lyrics they listen to is to ask them, "Would you want your child or younger sister (or brother) to listen to these words?" This one sentence puts everything into perspective. Even though they may feel the lyrics are acceptable and harmless to them, they often admit they would never let their sibling or child hear the same words. Often this one sentence opens the teen's mind in a way that nothing else can.

On Video Games

Our children are accountable for their behavior. Help them to be accountable for "wasting" time as well. We admit that our own children at one time were addicted to video games—before we began to see the damage they can cause to the child and to the family if no limits are set.

No one but you can decide what is right for your family. Observe your children as they engage in video games. Are they so absorbed that they get no physical exercise? Are grades suffering? How are their peer relationships? As you help your children become accountable for how they spend their time and the choices they make, it is important that your children have an understanding of all forms of media, including video games, and how they affect the entire family.

If Not from You, Then Who?

If you have no television or movie rules, set some today. Tell your teen why he or she cannot watch a particular show or "R" rated movie. A statement such as, "The values are not consistent with ours" says it all. The ultimate decision as to what influences your child is yours as parent. Set up media guidelines. Limit the amount of time your children spend on video games. Talk with your children and teach them how to make moral choices. More important, stay on top of what enters your child's mind.

The Higher the Pedestal, the Farther You Fall

The bottom line is that we are all accountable. We're held accountable for every action we make and every word we speak. We're personally responsible for what we watch on TV, what we read, the company we keep, the choices we make, whether we lie or cheat, and whether we uphold our values or give in to society's pleasures. As Christians, because Christ died and rose for us, we want to live as He did. We want to be accountable for our behavior—and we want it to be positive, honest, and forthright.

As you begin to make changes at the heart of your home, remember God never promised our lives would be without pain or hurt. There is no Bible verse that says when you own up to your behavior—right or wrong—everyone will cheer and throw loving arms around you. However, God does offer us acceptance, loving forgiveness, and strength to cope during the rough times—times when we have to admit we are wrong or have failed or hurt someone.

Remember the words of Paul: "Whether we are at home or away, we make it our aim to please Him" (2 Corinthians 5:9 RSV). And pleasing Him means modeling and teaching our children to live with the highest level of personal Christian responsibility.

⑤
CONTENTMENT

If we asked you what state you live in, you would immediately think of one of our nation's 50 sovereign units. If you are reading this on a challenging day, you might even think of the state of confusion! But if we asked the apostle Paul the same question, he would be thinking on a far different level. In Philippians 4:11, Paul wrote: "Not that I speak in respect of want: for I have learned, in whatsoever state I am, therewith to be content" (KJV).

The NIV translates verses 11 and 12 as: "I am not saying this because I am in need, for I have learned to be content whatever the circumstances. I know what it is to be in need, and I know what it is to have plenty. I have learned the secret of being content in any and every situation, whether well fed or hungry, whether living in plenty or in want." It sounds as if Paul lived in the state of contentment.

We admire Paul as he makes this proclamation, as if he has some supernatural power to deny himself what he wants or to be happy in all situations. Perhaps you have not connected his next words in verse 13 with verses 11 and 12. In verse 13, Paul reveals his secret: He is not some extraordinary man able always to deny himself of life's finest. His strength comes from the same source of power available to us. In the King James version, verse 13 reads: "I can do all things through Christ which strengtheneth me."

Paul certainly wasn't perfect and he probably wasn't always content, but he knew that contentment comes from a relationship with Jesus Christ and not from "stuffitis," a condition where the more you get, the more you want. Stuffitis wouldn't have done Paul much good between prison and shipwrecks. He understood his priorities.

A Personal Note

I thought it was just going to be another ordinary afternoon car ride with my 3-year-old (and recently potty-trained) daughter and her 7-year-old brother. But from somewhere in my son's theological mind came the question, "Mom, will there be any toys in heaven?"

Now, you know as Christian parents, we must stand ready to answer any question on any subject but to be honest, that one wasn't on my list! I managed to keep my composure and expertly say, "Stuart, heaven will be a place where we will always be happy because Jesus is there and He will take care of all our needs."

I know that may not be the most theologically accurate statement of all time, but I was pretty proud of it until he responded with, "I know that, Mom, but I just didn't know if that meant we would have toys."

I was only temporarily stunned and managed to come back with, "Son, if you think you will need toys, then God will take care of your needs."

As we continued our deep theological conversation, I started hearing this persistent little voice from the back seat trying to interrupt.

"But Mommy, but Mommy!"

"Yes, Emily, what is it, Sweetie?"

"But Mommy, will there be potties in heaven too?"

At that moment, Emily was more concerned about her needs, not her wants. A bathroom became a priority. I assured her that God would take care of her needs; and if she needed a potty, then it would be there. My answer seemed to bring her immediate contentment.

Ellen

Wouldn't life be simple if we all found contentment so easily? But the statistics tell a different story.

Kids with Money

After face-to-face interviews with 1,205 children nationwide, the Roper Youth Report indicates that children ages 8 to 17 have more weekly money to spend on themselves than in previous years. Preteens accumulate an average of $7.30 for weekly discretionary spending which is up from $6.00 in 1995. Teenagers ages 13 to 17 average $25.60 a week for spending money, a 51 percent increase over 1995's figure of $17.00.

In fact, spending by teenagers themselves has increased every year from 1953 to 1996. Even eight recessions and a drop in group size when Generation X became teens did not change the rate of spending. In 1980 alone, more than 29 million teenagers in this country spent just over $30 billion. Now, researchers put total annual teen spending at somewhere between $97.7 billion and $108 billion. All researchers agree that teen spending will continue to climb. It is estimated their spending will reach $136 billion by 2001. Where does their money go?

CLOTHING	34%
ENTERTAINMENT	22%
FOOD	16%
OTHER	28%

Is it wrong for our children and teens to have more money to spend? After all, everything costs more today. The key words here are *everything* and *more*. And it does cost money to buy everything and acquire more and more. If children and teens could distinguish their needs from their wants, many future common financial problems would be alleviated for them. However, Americans are cursed with an obsessive disorder we call "stuffitis." You might commonly call this *materialism* but it can apply to every area of our lives. In fact, when one area becomes obsessive, other areas seem to follow. We eat too much, we want too much, we buy too much, and we do too much. The sad result is that the more we acquire in any area, the more there is to take care of. And the more there is to take care of, the more time it demands to take care of what we accumulate, unless of course, we have so much that we lose respect for it and don't take care of it. Is it no wonder that financial concerns continue to be the most common cause of marital stress in America.

In order for you to fully understand how stuffitis works, look at the following real-life scenarios:

Scenario 1

Tim and Beth were both brought up in middle-class America. Tim's dad worked full-time and his mom worked part-time. Beth's dad worked full-time but her mom did not work outside the home. Both sets of parents started their married lives with very little after the war. It took years of hard work and living with little luxury to work their way up to the stable middle class. Both sets of parents put their kids through college.

Now Tim works full-time, and so does Beth, so they can afford their nice middle-class, suburban home, which is a little larger than the homes of their parents. Both of their children are in child care.

Problem: Many young couples think they must start off their marriage at the same standard of living it took their parents decades to work toward and enjoy. In order to achieve "the look of having arrived" they both must work and purchase many items on credit. Both adults are tired most of the time. Vacations are taken because they are part of the "looking good" package. The right kind of cars are bought and the right kind of clothes are worn.

What are the children learning? They are learning that acquiring the "right stuff" is the desired goal. Even if it is never said to their children, they will pick up the attitude that what you have is more important than who you are. They are learning that with enough acquired stuff you do not have to be honest about who or what you really are.

Scenario 2

Jim is an engineer with a national company. Elizabeth doesn't work outside the home. Jim was the first one in his family to graduate from college. Elizabeth dropped out when she became pregnant with their first child. Elizabeth reads everything she can about how children learn and what stimulates their thinking. She wants to make sure her children grow up to be successful. Jim works overtime to provide private schooling for their oldest child and preschool enrichment programs for their youngest. Elizabeth is pregnant with their third child.

While Jim works an average week of 60 hours and more, Elizabeth is constantly transporting children to soccer, ballet, computer class, and gymnastics. She is the room mother for her son's class at school and will serve on the PTA board for the coming year. She volunteers at the school two mornings a week.

Problem: Jim and Elizabeth want smart, successful children at any cost. Their children have little unstructured time to create, imagine, play freely outside, or learn to play independently. Bonding through simple family fun is sacrificed for the perfect family image through successful-looking children. What Jim and Elizabeth do not know is that they are exhausting themselves and exhausting their children. Constant activity can only assure us of fatigue and burnout.

What are the children learning? The children receive a loud and clear message that they *must* be smart and successful. At an early age, they understand there is no room for failure. They pick up the message that spending time sitting still, being quiet and reflective is not acceptable. It is difficult to be honest about who we are before God if we never sit still long enough to find out.

Scenario 3

Paul and Kim have one son, Eric, age 5. They are seriously concerned about the physical problems a growing number of Americans face. In order to stay healthy, they have completely revamped their lifestyle to include all natural foods, vitamins, and exercise. Both parents work. Eric is dropped off at a child care center before school each morning so Paul and Kim can squeeze in their workout time at the YMCA. Three evenings a week, Kim makes dinner for the boys and then heads out for an aerobics class. Eric participates in a different sport each season. He likes soccer best. Kim watches everything her son eats. His teacher has specific instructions about the foods Eric cannot eat. If he is allowed to play at a friend's house, before Kim leaves him, she reiterates the eating rules with Eric and the host parent.

Paul spends most weekends golfing or, if time allows, the family will bike together. Kim attends most of Eric's sporting events and Paul comes when his work schedule allows. Kim and Paul often tell each other how good they look. They each know how attractive they are to others.

Problem: While staying healthy and physically fit should be of concern to us all, it cannot take care of everything that is wrong in society. Becoming obsessed with physical fitness will not ensure that your child grows up healthy in all areas of life. Spending the majority of family time in separate dictated physical regimens does not allow for emotional bonding. If the family balanced their physical fitness with emotional and spiritual fitness, they would live a healthy life. It does not matter how physically fit you are; your child still needs and wants to hug you and to have you hug back.

What is the child learning? Eric is learning that taking care of his body is the most important goal in life. He is subtly learning that the body is not for hugging and loving, it is for fitness and looking good. He is learning that obsession is good if it is disguised as good health.

Scenario 4

Jenny is a single mom with three children, ages 9, 12, and 15. She manages to hold down an excellent and lucrative job. Adding her salary to the child support, she can provide her children with most of the necessities and some luxuries. Any extra time Jenny and the kids have is spent at church or with church friends. They are there on Sunday mornings, Sunday nights, and Wednesday nights, and Jenny attends the singles' Bible study on Thursday nights. She has just started leading a special year-long study for women that will meet on Sunday nights. It will require disciplined Bible study and outside reading and study. At the dinner table, she tries to steer the conversation to spiritual things and desperately desires her children to have their own quiet time every day.

Her younger kids get a little tired of going to church sometimes, but enjoy seeing their friends. Her teenager seems to be rebelling against going to church all the time, but Jenny thinks that is only natural at his age. She prays for her children constantly.

Problem: Christians are to be in the world but not of the world. Jenny has the last part figured out, but needs to allow for more time to work on the first part. We can become obsessed with spiritual things just as we can with anything else. God desires us to worship Him so we can gain the insight and strength to go out and share Him with others. If children are constantly attending church activities without other outlets, they may tire of going to church all the time. Spending more time at church or leading church activities will not wipe out our past or bring wholeness to our family. Gathering in fellowship with other believers and growing as Christians are wonderful if these factors are used as starting points for us to share the Gospel with our own family and friends who need Christ. Our faith is meant to be a springboard, not a crutch.

What are the children learning? The children are learning that the church can rob you of family time. In addition, if there is bitterness directed at the church, it will translate to anger toward God. They are learning that grace is something you obviously must work hard to earn instead of being a free, undeserved gift from God. They are learning that you deal with your problems by becoming spiritually busy.

Our obsessions are clearly manifestations of our lack of contentment. Our obsessions imprison our time, our money, our beliefs, our family, and our future. Even good things become dangerous when we allow them to become obsessive gods. You may not have found all of your lifestyle in any of the above scenarios, but perhaps you saw a little of it in several or all or them.

Where Does Contentment Start?

Obviously, it doesn't start in power. But where does it begin for each of us? If parents cannot find contentment, how can their children?

Let's go back to Paul. The secret of his contentment was in his relationship with Jesus Christ. And if we look at the life of Christ, we know that even the Savior of the world pulled away from the crowds and His disciples to find time to be with His Father. It is in the quiet, honest times with a loving God that He reveals to us who we are. In those moments, He gives us faith and direction. In those moments of quietness with the Creator, we gain strength for the journey. There is no pretense when we are in His presence. No accumulation of wealth or power or even spiritual knowledge makes a difference. God desires our love and honesty. He wants to meet us just as we are, no matter where we are.

Be still, and know that I am God. Psalm 46:10

Take the Simple Test

Many families are joining a movement toward a voluntary simplified lifestyle. The growth of the movement in the 1990s has earned it trend status. But it is not about a trend. People are deliberately choosing to determine their direction. They may not all be approaching their lifestyle change from a Christian perspective, but they know they want to slow down the merry-go-round for themselves and their children. They are finding that the pressure to accumulate things isn't getting them happiness. They are saying to their workload, activities, schedules, accumulation of things, credit cards, and most important, to themselves, "Enough is enough."

These people are among millions who are trading stress for simplicity. Reports of study after study name stress as a key factor contributing to such illnesses as heart disease, depression, anxiety disorders, asthma, allergies, and cancer. Buying more and more stress will only lead to the epitaph, "He did too much."

Most of the articles and books on simplifying your lifestyle do not promote one absolute prescription for de-stressing your world. Simplifying is different for each person and each family. Consider the following in making simplification decisions:

- *Discuss with your spouse and older children and teens what is really important to your family.*
- *Honestly decide together what areas of your life are out of control.*
- *Look at one area at a time and decide on definite steps to simplify your life and make more time for family and individual contentment.*
- *Read and listen to advice on how to take control.*
- *Seek the support of others who have made similar decisions.*

- *Start out slowly and experiment with what you can do without.*

These questions can help as you begin to experiment.

- *Is this really important to me?*
- *Do I truly enjoy this?*
- *Do I really need this?*
- *Does this cause stress and drain my energy?*
- *Does this cause me to hurry too much?*
- *What are healthier alternatives?*
- *How did I manage without this?*

What do you really want to pass on to your children? Sadly, we often perpetuate stress, out-of-control living, and a dependence on *stuff* for our contentment. Allow your children to experience a slower lifestyle that will promote satisfaction when they have their needs met instead of constantly desiring the things that will only increase their wants. "Keep in mind that whoever loves money never has money enough; whoever loves wealth is never satisfied with his income. This too is meaningless. As goods increase, so do those who consume them. And what benefit are they to the owner except to feast his eyes on them?" (Ecclesiastes 5:10–11).

Values Check

I Lead, You Follow

Think about how many times in a week you feel one of the following:

- *Overwhelmed*
- *Tired*
- *Frenzied*

- *Frustrated*
- *Overworked*

If any of the above feelings are a regular part of your week, then you need to take a good look at what the causes are and what you are willing to do to make your life less stressful. Write down what it would take you to truly feel contented. To help you take steps toward your own personal contentment, talk to people whom you admire and consider contented. Find out what their strategy is.

Arrange to spend part of a day alone with God. Try going to a favorite outdoor spot or a retreat setting. Read the following passages to help you examine your lifestyle:

- *Psalm 63:1–5*
- *Psalm 90:14*
- *Proverbs 19:23*
- *Isaiah 55:2*
- *1 Timothy 6:6–10*
- *Hebrews 13:5*

Seize the Opportunity

A contented lifestyle in no way assures you of an existence devoid of problems. Extreme problems and pestilence marked the apostle Paul's journeys. Paul learned that through Christ, he could be satisfied with circumstances beyond his control. He literally put trouble to work for him and seized a problem as an opportunity. Happiness triumphs over troubles. What are you modeling for your child?

Look at ways to control spending in order to simplify your life and pay off debt. Check off what you are currently doing to save:

— Deposit money each payday into your checking and savings accounts.

— Stick to a written spending plan and budget.

— Use a list when you grocery shop and try not to go more than once a week.

— Avoid carrying credit card balances.

— Use coupons.

— Dine out only once a week.

— Account for all cash spent at the end of the day.

You and I Lead Together

When you are contented with life, you want to share that with your child. You want him to know that part of your happiness comes from being his mom or dad.

- *Tell your child at least three times every day, "I love you."*

- *Give your child at least 30 minutes of your undivided time each day. Let him know that he is more important than telephone calls, pagers, computers, or doorbells.*

- *Play with your child. Go for walks. Try to see the world from his or her perspective. Ask God to help you discern how to pass on contentment to your child.*

- *Keep in mind that a contented child:*
  - Knows she is a special creation of God.
  - Feels loved and knows that he is lovable.
  - Is valued and develops a healthy self-esteem.
  - Understands the difference between needs and wants.

- Is grateful for what she has.
- Treats people and belongings with respect.
- Learns to listen to his own feelings and the feelings of others.
- Is easily pleased.
- Seeks to serve others.
- Is optimistic.

- *Learn more about your child's interests and gifts. What makes him feel good about himself?*

- *Find at least three positive aspects about your child every day and make sure to say them aloud.*

- *Start teaching money management early. Even older preschoolers can save their nickels and dimes to give to God, to missions, or to buy something special for themselves or someone else. Allow children to earn money with jobs around the house and yard. If you do not choose to give your child money for everyday jobs through allowances, then reward your child for special jobs. When a friend or relative has a birthday, encourage your child to use her own money to buy a gift or to use her creativity to make a gift and card.*

- *Save as a family for special occasions and for college. Start saving in advance for family vacations. Allow children and parents to put in money each week. Hold a family garage sale to make extra money.*

- *Contented people focus on others. Kids can learn that giving feels good. Decide on family projects that minister to others:*
  - A family mission trip
  - Donating clothes and toys to a homeless shelter
  - Adopting a senior adult in a nursing home
  - Befriending a refugee family with children

— Buying books for children without any
— When grocery shopping, ask your child to choose three cans of food to donate to a soup kitchen.

You Lead, I Follow

As you influence your child to find contentment in himself through his relationship with Christ and his concern for others, watch how he leads others to do the same. Compliment him when he takes the lead at church or school. However, carefully help him balance his leadership time with quiet time and family time.

Contented Teens? Is It Possible?

If it is true that happy adults have healthy self-esteem, then it is even truer for adolescents. Nothing challenges the confidence of boys and girls like the teen years. And nothing challenges the confidence of their parents like the teen years. Studies contend that parental influences during adolescence still make a difference.

Adolescents who do well tend to come from families where:

- *All members of the family communicate daily.*
- *Guidance on growing up is constantly shared.*
- *Kids are encouraged to share their thoughts and feelings in honest conversation.*
- *The family has traditional rituals and shared experiences.*
- *Family discipline, responsibilities, and expectations are clear and positive.*
- *The family demonstrates caring, sharing, and communication to solve problems.*
- *The family reacts to change well and shows flexibility.*

- *The family atmosphere is tolerant and accepting and provides for children to be themselves.*

Learning to manage his time and money will help your teen feel confident and content. Teenagers can, and often do, spend their own money for clothes and entertainment. Learning to save part of their money is essential for teens who plan to go on to college after high school. Before a teen leaves home, he should be able to handle his own checking and savings accounts. Refrain from encouraging your teen to apply for or accept credit cards.

There is a fine balance between helping your teen manage her time and allowing her to experience the consequences of mismanaged time. Younger teens need you to set boundaries, curfews, and study expectations. As teens get older, release more responsibility to them, but watch closely for overload. If your teen is experiencing high levels of stress and fatigue, or illness, you need to step in and set some new limitations.

A Personal Note

I know cable TV is dangerous. It introduces our children to questionable information that might not be suitable for them to learn. Such was the case in our home with my teenage daughter. One day after watching a cable channel, Emily came to me with quite a startling question.

"Mom, I've been watching one of those shows where they do really cool things to houses and yards. And I was wondering, would it be okay if my friends wrote all over my walls?"

"Excuse me?" was all I could get out of my mouth. "What did you just ask?"

"Yeah, they turned the walls into like a high school yearbook page and kids could write all over them. That would be so cool! Don't you think?"

You know, no matter how prepared you think you are, sometimes you are caught a little off guard.

I knew exactly how to steer around this one. I instructed her to ask my husband when he arrived home. I knew he would nip this in the bud. He would instantly say no, especially if she asked him after he came in from a long day.

You know, men, sometimes we just can't count on you! He told her that as long as they used non-permanent magic markers and nothing got on her carpet, he thought it would be okay. He said if it didn't turn out to be a good idea, we could just paint over it again.

Although it seemed very questionable at first, it has turned out to be great fun. Emily's room is complete with cathedral ceilings, so kids have to stand on chairs and the top bunk to get really up there, but they do! It is quite a conversation piece! Best of all, she cleans her room so friends can come in and sign her wall.

Our teenage next-door neighbor claimed one of the walls for himself and came over 30 days straight to write something on it. There are telephone numbers,

Shakespeare quotes, Scripture verses, and little hidden messages around doors, in closets, and behind mirrors.

And just like a high school yearbook, many friends write messages offering support and encouragement. Every night when Emily goes to bed, she is surrounded by the support of all her friends.

Ellen

Walls of Faith

Walls of support give a teen a foundation of confidence in who she is. When your teen knows that you love her unconditionally, her walls are strengthened for when she must take a stand against something questionable. Support from other caring adults, such as church leaders and teachers, will further strengthen her walls. It is in the church and home that children and teenagers hear about the secret to a contented life. They need to see the abundant Christian life modeled by the adults who care about them. They need to see adults who are contented in Christ no matter what obstacles they must face.

In addition, they need Christian friends who will remind them of God's love for them. We can't pick the friends we want our children to choose. But we can talk to them about the value of strong Christian peers. We can open our home to their friends during childhood and on through their teen years. Birthday parties, church fellowships, and informal times, when friends can just drop by will allow you to see who your child or teen is choosing as a friend. If your teen's friends are always invited and welcomed in your home, you will learn more about your child and what she thinks as you listen to her interact with friends.

Surround your teenagers with honest, Christlike love as you ride through the ups and downs of adolescence with them. Ride a little closer in the beginning and then allow them some driving room to maneuver through as they mature, knowing that you are there when they need you. More important, remind them that God will never leave them nor forsake them.

Contentment escapes most of America today. As the fast technological pace continues toward the next century, contentment will be lost if we don't start making changes now in ourselves and our families. In reminding your kids of God's love for them, you will be reminding yourself of the same.

No matter how much we'd like a guarantee, there is no warranty that public figures and other role models will demonstrate honest, Christian contentment. The devil and our sinful flesh will feed our discontentment. But with thanksgiving and gratitude for God's blessings and gifts, we can learn to be satisfied with what we have. Perhaps William Henry Channing summed it up best in *My Symphony*:

> *To live content with small means; to seek elegance rather than luxury, and refinement rather than fashion; to be worthy, not respectable; and wealthy, not rich; to study hard, think quietly, talk gently, act frankly; to listen to stars and birds, to babes and sages, with open heart; to bear all cheerfully, do all bravely, await occasions, hurry never. In a word, to*

let spiritual, unbidden and unconscious, grow up through the common. This is to be my symphony.

May this be your symphony too!

⑥
BENEVOLENCE

"She doesn't care about anything."

"He's so apathetic about his life and family."

"*Self-absorbed* describes her accurately."

"He's so sullen and moody and she has no goals in life."

Sullen. Moody. Self-absorbed. Apathetic. Uncaring. Do these words describe anyone you know? Surprisingly, these are words parents used to describe their teenagers at a recent parenting workshop. Shannon, a single parent of two, confided that perhaps her 16-year-old daughter was seriously depressed because she "lies on her bed every day after school with the door closed and the music blasting. She has no purpose or motivation for life." Another parent, John, experienced the same with his 13-year-old son and asked how to encourage him to get outside himself. "After school Jeremy sits in front of his computer and plays video games until dinnertime. He's distant, sullen, and has no interest in anything but being alone. Even when friends come to hang out with him, he makes up excuses to be alone and retreats to his room."

Igniting Passion

Apathy, moodiness, and lack of purpose in life can be symptoms of depression; childhood depression is serious and mandates serious attention. Yet apathy, moodiness, and lack of purpose are also signs of those who lack passion and compassion in their lives.

The National Institute of Mental Health in Bethesda, Maryland, estimates that more than 1.5 million American children under 18 are seriously depressed, and the American Academy of Child and Adolescent Psychiatry puts the number at more than twice the Institute's estimate. The real number may be higher still, and it is almost certainly growing.

Marcus Aurelius said, "A man's life is what his thoughts make it." For Christians, it's difficult to think of our relationship with God and giving to others when we are so preoccupied with our own selfish wants and needs. Perhaps you have realized that our hurried society destroys two fundamental keys of human wholeness: intimacy and transcendence. We all need intimacy to love and feel loved or connected. We are also not complete without transcendence—spiritual experiences that enable us to feel godly love and trust and that inspire us to reach out and help others.

You Can't Take It with You

Jacob's situation is one you are probably familiar with: too much work, not enough personal time, too much stress, no communication with his wife or children, not enough meaningful experiences, and so on. And Jacob also unhappily acknowledged, "In trying so hard to make a living, I have neglected my spiritual life."

Aren't we all like that at times? We get so caught up in the pressures of our goal-oriented society trying to provide "stuff" for our families that the only measurement we have of personal fulfillment lies in wealth and status. In our free time—what little there is—we spend hours staring at the television, surfing the Internet, or burying our heads in mass-market novels. Yet a society infatuated with material success and results offers no solace to the harried. In the midst of our struggle to get ahead, we miss what is most important in life—spiritual wholeness.

Why Is Your Child Lonely?

Researchers at Carnegie Mellon University have found that people who spend even a few hours a week online experience higher levels of depression and loneliness than they would have if they used the computer less frequently. The two-year study called "HomeNet" concluded that the interactive medium may be no more socially healthy than older mass media, such as television.

Harvard Medical School conference speakers recently echoed that people with a deep sense of spirituality are able to stop focusing on themselves and to start focusing on others—an altruistic attitude that promotes better mental and physical health. This may be compared to the so-called French Paradox. Researchers have found that in spite of the traditional French diet, the French live longer and have a lower rate of heart disease. Perhaps the major difference is cultural. The social support of the French may protect them from their diet as occasions for friends and family are plentiful, helping them to receive comfort for their souls.

How does benevolence relate to improved health and self-esteem? New studies show that when you bridge social isolation through altruistic measures instead of dwelling on your own problems, your outlook on life will soar. For parents, this means that you can help change apathy and lack of purpose to action and passion about life! Some people diagnosed with depression in our society may be instead *spiritually* depressed—that is, living day to day without a purpose and passion to give to others.

The Heart of Our Faith

Isn't life barren when you only focus on yourself? Dennis Campbell said, "We are guilty of giving our kids too much to live with but not enough to live for!" Christianity can dramatically change this by giving both meaning and purpose to life. At the heart of Christian love is self giving, and part of coming to maturity as a Christian is identifying the unique talents and abilities God has given you and using them for His glory. Remember, it is God who gave us our talents. In fact, all we have comes from God. We dare not imagine that we can take pride in our accomplishments—no matter how extraordinary they may be. Rather, we must get on our knees daily and say with joyful and thankful hearts, "Thank You, Lord!"

Throughout the Bible are references to both our individual responsibility to God and our responsibility to the community of faith. We are commissioned to care for the least of these, feed the hungry, and clothe the naked. Jesus tells us to "love your neighbor as yourself" (Matthew 19:19) and "Do to others as you would have them do to you" (Luke 6:31). As a parent concerned with raising honest children, teach your child these obligations and help him move from being self-centered to being others-centered, using his special talents. Because God is the giver of all talents, we are called to use them in service to the world.

The parable of the talents (Matthew 25:14–30) paints an accurate portrayal of what can happen when you hide your abilities. The king gave to each of three servants a gift of money and when he returned he asked to see what they had done with it. The servant who had been given five talents had doubled his gift. The master put him in charge of many things. The second servant had been given two talents. He too doubled his gifts and was put in charge of many things. But the other servant, out of fear, had buried his gift in the ground. The master was highly displeased. The poor servant had his gift taken away.

Roots and Wings

So, the question is: what do we do with what we have? Being "rooted in the world" by learning benevolent behavior at home will allow your child to have "wings" when he matures and leaves the nest. While thoughts are important, it is the action—putting feet to our Christian faith—which really touches lives. God has given us all these wonderful abilities and talents, and He means for us to use them benevolently—serving in the world, as teachers, preachers, pastors, physicists, clerks, and more. Being benevolent or serving others means giving of ourselves for the benefit of others. Interestingly, while benevolence is centered on helping others, we are also greatly blessed in return.

Teaching your child benevolence is not something that can be done in one day! Rather, it must be nurtured from early childhood. How you lovingly hold him as a baby, appropriately respond to his needs as a toddler, answer his many childhood questions, and listen patiently to his trials during teenage years—all help to reinforce this value.

Our goal as Christian parents is to nurture the child so he may experience God's love, with a personal faith in Jesus Christ as the expected result. This personal faith gives children a sense of belonging as the Bible teaches the child that he or she is of ultimate worth. Christianity taught in the family gives children self-esteem; they become sensitized to the perils of humanity and can respond with empathy to injustice in the world. The idea that "I am loved, therefore I can love others" is a cherished outcome of our faith in Jesus Christ.

Plant Compassionate Roots

> *"Dear children, let us not love with words or tongue but with actions and in truth."*
> *1 John 3:18*

We make a living by what we get out of life, but we make a life by what we give. Benevolence starts by putting "feet to faith" right where you are. Being a Christian witness starts as children learn to reach out beyond themselves and to minister to others—siblings, parents, friends, neighbors—in a way that will touch them in their own lives. As our children begin to emerge spiritually, they may seek to help others more in a benevolent manner—authentic faith results in showing love to others. They may take such actions as helping the new child at school, being kinder to a sibling, offering to help around the house without being asked, or taking cookies to a neighbor who is ill. As your child watches you care for grandparents or other family members, neighbors who are ill or in crisis, friends who need a helping hand, and "the least of these" in your community, she will learn to do the same. But keep in mind, while good intentions to help others or to be benevolent are admirable, unless action takes place, they have no meaning.

It is difficult for busy moms and dads to follow through with kind deeds when their day is crammed with wiping noses, carpooling to Little League games, reading spelling words aloud, or picking up crumbs under the kitchen table. But the following steps will show how just a few minutes each day can give enough time to teach benevolent giving.

Call Them by Name

> *"The sheep listen to his voice. He calls his own sheep by name and leads them out." John 10:3b*

The Bible challenges Christians to know one another's names and care for one another. We can mentally picture the worn shepherd keeping track of all the furry sheep, large and small, young and old, as they enter the pasture for grazing. Most shepherds verify that if one sheep becomes lost or hurt along the way, he will leave the flock to find or comfort it.

To be benevolent and care for others, we are called upon to be shepherds. We must know all about those around us—their feelings, fears, likes and dislikes, dreams and goals. Only by knowing others can we minister to them in a way that really touches their lives. Not only are we commissioned to teach the Word of God, we are also instructed to heal the wounds, celebrate the victories, and provide opportunities for our children to respond to God's love.

Christ believed in the principle that a small group of well-trained disciples could permeate a larger group in much the same way that a little yeast in the dough affects the whole loaf (Luke 13:21). Jesus not only taught this principle, He also put it into practice in the training of the Twelve. It was through the investment of Himself in an intimate, instructive, purposeful relationship that Jesus equipped the Twelve. Through the course of a few years, He trained them by indelibly stamping their lives with a model of ministry they could not forget.[11]

As Christians, we also indelibly stamp lives within our families, our neighborhood, our community, and our world. Our concern for others must be so intimate, so full of selfless love, that people know we are authentic.

Demonstrate Caring

"Truly, I say to you, as you did it not to one of
the least of these, you did it not to Me."
Matthew 25:46 RSV

"Who cares?" is a popular phrase today. Yet the words "who cares" have a much deeper meaning in our world, for they reflect much of the emptiness and apathy toward others that many people feel. Developing caring or benevolent qualities in your child takes years of patience and nurturance; yet the rewards are to be found years later as the child's attitude develops from the negative "who cares" to the more Christlike attitude of "I care."

Keep in mind as you teach benevolence that caring is a learned trait, not an inborn sense. As a child is spoken to in a loving manner, is given limits to his actions, and is able to share in a family situation where genuine caring is shown, he is more likely to develop attributes such as patience, kindness, and consideration.

Teaching a child to care for those around him is not a simple task. Caring is a learned process developed through interaction with loving caregivers who take time to be with the child, talk with the child, and even say no at times. A child will remember the moments you demonstrate care and concern as you teach him what Christian love is all about.

You show caring by

- *Spending quality time together. Listen to your child's fears and frustrations, and help him feel secure in your love for him.*

- *Listening with compassion. When feelings and thoughts are poured out and real listening occurs, your child will feel loved and understood.*

- *Making eye contact while conversing. Each time you look away while listening to your child, communication breaks down.*

- *Asking questions. Get the facts straight before offering an opinion.*

- *Being sensitive. Even if the topic seems irrelevant, don't shrug off your child.*

- *Responding reflectively. This does not mean that you have to agree with your child always, but you do need to accept what your child is saying as valid.*

- *Listening to nonverbal communication. Look beyond the body language to what your child is really saying.*

- *Becoming an active listener. Hearing is passive. Listening is active because it involves mental effort and attention. Respond with understanding. Try to identify with what the child is saying.*

- *Being approachable. Accept the subject the child is discussing and react objectively.*

- *Using gentle touch to show you care. This nonverbal form of love can be used with young and old alike as you interact in an affirming way—no words, just gentle hugs, pats, and caresses. Remember how Jesus reached out with gentle, caring hands, touching cold and empty lives with His power.*

- *Identifying and sharing your personal feelings. Let your child know that you have feelings too. When he defies you or talks back, openly say, "You hurt me when you do that." Or when she brings you a colorful picture, say, "That makes me feel so good inside."*

- *Helping him consider how others might feel. If a situation occurs where the child demonstrates behavior that would not be considered caring, help the child relate the incident to his own life.*

- *Explaining to the child why you do random acts of kindness for others. If you take a neighbor flowers or food when he is ill, let your child know you did this because you care for that person. When you volunteer to keep a friend's children so she can have time out, tell your child why Christians are urged to help others.*

- *Being considerate of your child's feelings. Don't compare him or his abilities to others. This comparison only destroys the self-image necessary for confident, caring living.*

- *Realizing that your child is unique and fits into God's plan for being special. Help him find his unique gifts and talents and build these strengths up verbally to him and to others. If your child is helpful during the day, tell the family about it. If the child brings home a report or picture from school, take time to discuss it and comment on the talents the child has.*

- *Saying no and being firm but kind. Discipline and firmness also are evidence of caring. Help your child understand that you are saying no because you care; you are punishing him because of your love for him. It is often difficult for a child to understand the limits and consequences of his behavior. Yet if the parent is consistent with discipline, a child will sense caring and concern.*

A child learns caring mainly through watching the way you react to others. If you are inconsistent in showing concern for others, expect your child to be also. If you

have a lot of anger, frustrations, and other negative emotions, your child will also. On the other hand, if you
demonstrate love and caring toward others, your child
will probably pick up on this attitude. How you handle
neighbor relationships, family matters, and giving in your
community reinforces priorities that you have spoken of
as being important in your own life.

Your ultimate goal is to send your children into the
world knowing they will live each day with caring and
compassion. As they focus on loving others as Christ loves
them, they will do well.

Communicate Compassion

*You yourselves have been taught by God to love
each other. 1 Thessalonians 4:9*

Compassion is the ability to feel with another person, and what a wonderful asset a sense of compassion is
in the family! There is a story about two brothers who
were spending their last days together in a nursing home.
The brother in the bed closest to the window was warm,
talkative, outgoing, optimistic, and altogether very socia-
ble. The brother next to the door was blind, negative, and
quite lonely.

One day the brother next to the door asked the
brother next to the window to describe for him the things
that were going on outside. The brother next to the window took great delight in doing so. He described colorful
flowers bursting into bloom and delicate hummingbirds
feeding from the buds; he told how the mothers were
pushing babies in strollers and children were laughing on

the playground. This became a daily ritual as the jovial brother next to the window described to his blind brother the flurry of activity outside. The brother who was blind lived for these reports from outside.

But one day the sensitive, extroverted brother next to the window died, and his bed was taken by another man. "Would you please describe for me," asked the surviving brother next to the door, "what is going on outside our window?" The new roommate looked out the window in puzzlement and then looked back at the man, saying, "I don't see what good it would do, my friend. There is nothing outside this window except a dirty brick wall."

This story illustrates how God calls families to come together and "feel with" one another. God gives us compassion. What about in your family? Does someone have a stumbling block you can help with? Is there a member who is experiencing conflict, and you can offer empathy? What about someone who may be bitter from past failures? Can you help him see God's plan for his life?

In Paul's letter to the Ephesians, he writes, "It was He who gave some to be apostles, some to be prophets, some to be evangelists, and some to be pastors and teachers, to prepare God's people for works of service, so that the body of Christ may be built up until we all reach unity in the faith and in the knowledge of the Son of God and become mature, attaining the whole measure of the fullness of Christ" (Ephesians 4:11–13).

The amazing affirmation that Paul makes is that all of these differences are given to us to help us build one another up to maturity and to grow up into love. It is when we push and tug against each other in the family that we begin to discover who we are; we begin to grow into the persons God intended. It is when we compassionately reach out to family members "even though" that we are blessed.

Encourage Empathy and Tolerance

What Would Jesus Do?

An honest child who maintains high personal standards and who knows right from wrong is tolerant of others. As you show consideration in the family, your child will model your attitude toward her peers. Empathy involves caring for someone else to the point that you know how he feels, which leads to altruism. When we really feel what someone is going through, we want to reach out to him and help him. Children learn to have empathy as parents give emotional feedback, either showing pleasure or displeasure to their actions or speech.

Watch for signs that demonstrate your child is not accepting her peers. Talk openly about the potential in all of God's children, and observe your child at play to make sure the rules of tolerance are being followed. We often lean on the phrase, "How would you feel if someone did that to you?" to encourage acceptance of all God's people. Better still, ask your pastor for a *What Would Jesus Do?* bracelet, or purchase one at a Christian bookstore. This visible reminder is worn each day by men and women around the world to help believers remember to consider their faith before making choices. Once a child is able to react with empathy toward others, you can feel assured that the message of truth is being carried out into his or her world.

Empathy builds on self-awareness: the more open we are to our own emotions, the more skilled we will be in reading feelings. Empathy can be seen in the youngest child, even traced to infancy. Virtually from the day they are born, infants are upset when they hear another infant crying—a response some see as the earliest precursor of empathy.

You can develop a child's ability to empathize with others through daily experiences. As your child interacts with others and experiences conflict, ask:

1. What made you want to do that?

2. What if someone did that to you?

3. How would that make you feel?

4. How would you want a friend to treat you?

5. Would your feelings then change?

6. What can you do to apologize to your friend?

7. What would Jesus do in this situation?

You can help teach these values by role playing situations with your child. Create a situation that may not be fair or that may be unkind, and let your child discuss how he or she would act. When we were growing up, a popular children's magazine had a regular cartoon series that depicted two boys with contrasting behaviors and attitudes. One boy represented the "good guy," while the other boy acted in rebellion and anger. Children can identify with both individuals, but the family must encourage the correct way to treat others.

If your child acts like a bully around others, don't allow this to continue. No one should be allowed to put someone else down—for any reason. If you need to punish your child for such behavior, do so, then talk openly about how that person must have felt. Get the message across that God's plan for the world includes acceptance, compassion, and loving our neighbor as we love ourselves.

Teach Sharing

"Find out how much God has given you and from it take what you need; the remainder which you do not require is needed by others."
Augustine

"It's mine!" These are probably the two most frequently used words of a toddler or preschooler at play. If you observe children at play, it often seems that most little ones are born selfish. A young child's possessions are almost a part of himself. But the process of sharing demands a new type of self awareness. If the child is uncertain of his limits, he usually will be unwilling to give up his toys which are an extension of himself.

Values Check

I Lead, You Follow

- *Talk with your child about possessions in the family. Show the child your hairbrush, radio, shoes, and bed, then point out possessions in his room. Explain that everyone has certain possessions while you offer to "share" something with him.*

You and I Lead Together

- *When a friend is over, make sure both children have a special toy to share. Sharing is most frustrating for young children when there is only one "prized" toy.*

- *Use a timer to let children know when they must share the toy with another child. When the timer goes off, the children use this as a signal to give the toy to a friend.*

You Lead, I Follow

- *If there is extreme conflict about a favorite toy when friends are playing, put the toy away for a period of time and get the children interested in another activity.*

- *Realize that this intense self-centered stage will not last forever, and try to remain loving and calm as you deal with the young child's aggressions and frustrations.*

Reaching Out beyond the Family

"It is more blessed to give than to receive."
Acts 20:35

The elementary years are the perfect time to encourage benevolence with your child. Children of this age know what is right even though most parents would argue that they do not always *do* what is right. Elementary-age children are concerned with fairness and are conscientious about helping others, but they still may not be very helpful at home. And most elementary-age children like to improve social conditions. (Note: We did not say sibling conditions!) Realize the compassionate nature of this age, and incorporate into your family activities ways to teach your child to give to the less fortunate.

Values Check

I Lead, You Follow

- *Talk about giving to those who are in need. Go through your child's closet, toy box, and shelves and talk about giving away any unwanted toys, puzzles, cassette tapes, stuffed animals, or even quality clothing.*

- *Read Scripture verses aloud that present good models of giving. Read about the boy who shared his lunch (John 6:1–13) and the poor widow's offering (Luke 21:1–3) from a Bible storybook. Ask your child to name some specific ways he can show love by giving to others.*

You and I Lead Together

- *Call a volunteer organization in your community. Volunteer to help distribute food, clothing, or toys one Saturday when your child is out of school.*

- *Ask your pastor if you can help with local mission programs. Your local church may also have special programs for the needy, such as a toy or food drive, and could use extra help.*

- *Ask your pastor for the name of a shut-in at church. With your assistance, let your child make a card and plate of decorated cookies. Take these to the shut-in and plan to spend a few minutes enjoying fellowship.*

- *Take your child to a nursing home. Children like to feel important, and your child will feel even more blessed when she learns that many of these people have no immediate family to visit them.*

You Lead, I Follow

- *Encourage random acts of kindness. Teach your child to put "feet to faith" and be a good Samaritan as you challenge him to do random acts of kindness each day. Explain to your child that acts of kindness are as common as a cold and can be "caught" just as easily.*

Suggested Random Acts of Kindness

- Taking her plate to the kitchen after dinner
- Making his sister's bed
- Doing a chore without being reminded
- Walking a neighbor's dog after school
- Washing dishes for the family
- Taking out the trash without being asked
- Reading to a younger brother or sister
- Playing with a child who seems lonely
- Telling a friend about Jesus
- Praying for a friend
- Writing a thank you note to a good friend
- Giving a word of encouragement to someone who is worried
- Smiling at the new child at school
- Offering to help the teacher without being asked

Altruism and Teens

"Faith without deeds is useless." James 2:20

Millions of teens today are preparing for a future of helping others. Clubs such as Youth Against Cancer, Amnesty International, the Environmental Club, the Volunteer Club, and Youth for Christ serve as clearing-houses as middle and high school students get involved in something greater than self. These clubs have replaced social clubs or pep squads that teens migrated to a decade ago, perhaps showing that teens are looking for more than a good time as they grow up; they want purpose in life.

Volunteering offers many benefits such as:
— Giving a greater purpose in life
— Teaching compassion and empathy for others
— Helping place the focus on something greater than self
— Boosting self-esteem and confidence
— Giving life experiences

Where Do You Turn?

Volunteer opportunities exist almost anywhere people need services and funds are limited. Many large cities have a volunteer agency (Volunteers in Action, Voluntary Action Center, Volunteer Bureau) that places willing people in different positions and services after an initial screening of talents and time. Large institutions and hospitals have personnel who do the volunteer placement, and usually have special clubs or groups just for older elementary or teen volunteers. You may also call the guidance counselor at your child's school and ask for information on summer volunteering.

Where to Find Volunteer Opportunities

- *Doctor's offices*
- *Hospitals*
- *Nursing homes*
- *Churches*
- *Community organizations*

- *Hot line and crisis centers*
- *Charitable organizations (Red Cross, United Way)*
- *Halfway houses*
- *Political campaigns*
- *YMCA, YWCA*
- *Children's homes*
- *Schools and day care centers*
- *Zoos*

God Calls Us to Put Feet to Faith

As parents it is difficult to be available to heed God's call when days are filled with kids, carpools, commitments, and chaos. Nonetheless, evangelism for our Lord can only take place when we care for others using that selfless love Jesus taught or, to put it simply, by putting feet to faith. Teaching your child neighbor-love will strengthen her faith in a benevolent God and will serve as a genuine and honest spiritual witness to those around her.

⑦
FORGIVENESS

While forgiving those who have wronged us may be contrary to our nature, in order for growth and reconciliation to occur, forgiveness must take place. When parents learn to forgive, children can be taught how to forgive. Parents who understand grace raise children who understand grace. The Gospel message, the Good News, is that it is never too late to experience forgiveness in your family—no matter how old you are or how old your children are or how devastated your family life may be. God gives us His grace always—unconditionally—though we in no way deserve it. We are sinful by nature yet Jesus took upon Himself our sinfulness on the cross. That's *amazing* grace!

A Personal Note

I have never really known my mother. She left our family when we were small. We would see her from time to time, but eventually she stopped coming altogether. Several years later, we heard that she had died of complications caused by alcoholism. My two younger sisters and I lived with our father who was devoted to us and loved us. He dedicated every spare minute to us, and I know it wasn't easy for a single parent to hold down a job and raise three children.

While I was in seminary, I did a quarter's residency at Emory Hospital in Atlanta, Georgia. We had daily evaluation sessions, and one day we were sharing about the importance of family in our lives. As the discussion moved around the group, touching and moving stories were being shared about mothers and how important they were to children. When it came my turn, I had to admit that my mother did not play a large part in my life and that I really didn't care to remember much about her. The memories I did have were very painful to tell.

One occurred when I was very young. As a preschooler, I was playing with matches in our backyard and set a vacant lot on fire. As punishment, my mother burned the ends of all my fingers with the matches until they blistered. I remembered another time, when she ran away, my father took us with him to find her and bring her back home. After we found her, he talked her into getting into the car with us, but on the way home she jumped out of the moving car. The picture of seeing her rolling down the embankment is imprinted in my mind and is as painful as if it just happened yesterday. I remember my mother getting back in the car all scratched, bloody, and dirty. And I remember feeling so alone and frightened.

At that point in my story, some students in the group were crying, and so was I. But then I remembered something that happened when I was about 5 years old. We were living with relatives in Indiana while my father was in school, and I recalled my mother playing the piano at family gatherings. I'll never forget how everyone stood around her in awe while she played and how her long, graceful hands went up and down the keys in a melodic ecstasy. Later, when I began my musical studies at age 13, some of my relatives said I inherited my musical abilities from my mother. I went on to receive numerous piano scholarships for college and graduated with a degree in music before going on to seminary.

This didn't mean much to me until that day at the hospital, when my supervisor observed the ironic beauty in the situation. The very person who deserted our family when we needed her, who had abused me and caused our family untold pain, was the very one responsible for the most precious gift I had: my music.

Although my mother was dead, I reconciled with her that cold, rainy day at Emory Hospital, and I learned that even as much as I wanted to forget my mother, God wanted me to forgive her and to be thankful for her. In spite of the painful memories I associated with my mother, I now acknowledge her, thank her, and love her for the gift she unknowingly shared with me—the gift of music.

Bob

Freedom!

The beginning of freedom is not democracy or war or a flag. It is forgiveness. Without forgiveness, we are imprisoned in anger, resentment, and fear. Nothing can rob us more of the joys of the abundant life than failure to forgive. But nothing can unchain us from emotional pain and pressure like forgiveness. When we understand God's forgiveness through Jesus, then we are truly free to begin to live.

The sad reality is that many men and women begin marriage and parenthood still in chains. Every time they want to reach out to a spouse or to a child, the chains hold them down. The chains keep them afraid of trusting again. And in the process of fighting to stay chained up, they end up chaining their own children.

As you read through this chapter, honestly examine your memories and actions of the past. Evaluate how they are influencing your present and your child's future. God stands ready to forgive us any time we ask Him, and He longs to help us forgive others. An honest child is one who understands that the Gospel begins with forgiveness and salvation sets us free.

The Master's Plan

Sometimes we get tired of being role models. But it just comes with the parenting territory. Actually, it comes with the kingdom territory. Remember, your child's view of God is based on how you relate to her. To teach forgiveness, parents must ask for forgiveness when we have wronged our child, forgive him when he has wronged us, and demonstrate to him how to forgive others.

"Be kind and compassionate to one another, forgiving each other just as in Christ God forgave you." Ephesians 4:32

A Personal Note

As a parent, one of the hardest times to keep your cool is with your teenager. And usually it's through fault of my own, not my son's or daughter's. Sometimes, I don't really say hurtful things to them, but I voice reactionary words that stay with them.

As the new school year started, Emily began to tell me about her new teachers at church and school. She was upset about one of them. I took up the offense with her. I began to list the traits about this particular teacher that I didn't care for at all. As a mother I was not sure she was always the kind of role model I wanted my daughter to be around. I emphatically told Emily that I would speak to those in authority about the situation.

A good and bad characteristic about God is that He can be a pest! When He starts working on you and bothering you, He just doesn't let up. That is what happened. He started poking around on my heart while I was trying to put on make-up the next day. He knew I wasn't going anywhere until the job was completed! Little thoughts ran through my head like, "What if the teacher in question is exactly whom God has called and chosen to teach my daughter this year? What if it is this teacher who will make the most impact on her Christian life through all her teen years? What if this teacher needs to be in this specific teaching role so she can learn something from my daughter?" Who was I to condemn before I gave God the opportunity to freely work in my daughter's life and in this teacher's life?

I knew what I had to do. I asked God to forgive my reactionary, selfish, judgmental outburst in front of Emily. I prayed for Emily and the prospective teacher. I asked Emily to forgive my reaction and used the questions God brought to my mind to discuss the possibilities with her that evening.

Ellen

Q. What can you do when you are the one who has wronged your child?

A. Talk to God. Thank Him for such a wonderful child, one who will forgive you and love you unconditionally, no matter how you act. Ask God to forgive you and keep in mind that He promises to forgive for Jesus' sake every time you ask Him. Think about what you can do differently next time. Making a better plan can keep you from making the same mistake again. Now comes the hard part. Tell your child, "I'm sorry for the way I acted. I was wrong. I asked God to forgive me and He did. Now, I need to ask you to forgive me." Asking your child for forgiveness is a humbling but intimately rewarding experience. In order to be forgiven, you have to ask someone to forgive you. You must ask with a spirit of true repentance. We learn that from King David in Psalm 51.

"But You are a forgiving God, gracious and compassionate, slow to anger and abounding in love." Nehemiah 9:17a

When Your Child Is Wrong

"I love you, but I don't love what you did." This is extremely important to say to a child because it tells him you disapprove of his actions, and not of him. And when you separate the child from the action, it is much easier to forgive and not stay angry with him.

You know the scene. A similar one has probably occurred at your home. Your son has just broken the precious, antique vase given to you by your great-grandmother. He stands there, baseball in hand, the color quickly draining from his face. Is it okay to let him know you are upset and disappointed about the incident? Sure it is, but at the same time, he also needs to know you will forgive what happened if he asks. The conversation might go like this:

Dad: Okay, Son, please tell me exactly what happened.

Son: I was rolling my baseball, and it bounced up and hit the vase.

Dad: Son, tell me the rule about baseballs and the house.

Son: I can throw the baseball anytime I'm outside, and away from the house.

Dad: Did you follow the rule?

Son: No, Sir.

Dad: How do you think I feel now?

Son: Angry.

Dad: Yes, Son. I'm angry and sad. Tell me what you can do the next time you're carrying a baseball in the house.

Son: Keep it in my glove until I get outside. Dad, I'm really sorry I wasn't more careful.

Dad: Keeping it in your glove is a good idea. I am angry at what you did and sad that the vase was broken. You were wrong. But I love you and I forgive you.

What did Dad do? He asked his son to

1. Tell him what he had done.

2. Remind him of their rule.

3. Understand how the broken vase made him feel.

4. Create a plan to use the next time.

Before the conversation was finished, Dad made sure his son knew he was loved and forgiven. Is it necessary to immediately tell your child he's forgiven? No. If you are too angry or emotional, it might take more time for you to cool down. Saying, "I forgive you" when your face is still red might not be the most convincing. If you need to, assure your child of your love and then tell him you need to think about this and talk to him later.

It is critical that your child knows you love him and you have forgiven him. Holding a grudge against a child and not forgiving his actions causes a child to feel

- **Fear**—*The child who lives in fear of an angry, unforgiving adult can become overly withdrawn.*
- **Shame**—*The child who withdraws and feels unable to express his emotions can repress his emotions, which can build until he is overly stressed.*
- **Frustration**—*The child who lives in fear of an unforgiving adult feels the weight of the world on his shoulders, but his shoulders are not big enough to carry such a load.*

These children may express their emotions in explosive or violent ways that ultimately can harm others or themselves.

Some parents believe if they forgive the child they can't punish her for the disobedience. On the contrary, your child needs to be held accountable for the rules and the consequences. Make sure she is aware of what the rules and consequences are for disobedience before she disobeys. If necessary, follow through with consequences for your child's actions. Explain the reason. Tell her what she did was wrong and that you forgive her, but because she purposely disobeyed the rule, you have to follow through with the consequences. This will help her know you love her and forgive her, but you care enough about her to help her learn control.

John Unger, pastor of Richmond Park Mennonite Brethren Church in Brandon, Man., helps differentiate between what forgiveness is and what it isn't. He says that is it not saying to the other person, "It's okay. It doesn't matter." According to Unger, if it didn't matter, then forgiveness wouldn't be necessary. It matters.

Unger believes forgiveness is an act of letting go of the pain, anger, or resentment against the other person. It is a process of discovering layer after layer of feelings, which take time to discover and then to recover.

> *Then Peter came to Jesus and asked, "Lord, how many times shall I forgive my brother when he sins against me? Up to seven times? Jesus answered, "I tell you, not seven times, but seventy-seven times." Matthew 18:21–22*

When Others Wrong You

It will be hard for our children to believe we can forgive them or God can forgive them if they see we cannot forgive others. There is a fine line to walk in "hating the sin and loving the sinner." We must be careful that we don't take up an offense against someone who has wronged us or with whom we disagree. Sometimes we use the cause of Christ to further our own causes of anger or fear. We champion our own selfish causes and say we are protecting God's causes.

Children are smart and intuitive. They sense their parents' attitudes toward others. What are they hearing about forgiveness? Can they count to 77 yet?

Jesus set the example for us when He cried out to God, "Father, forgive them, for they do not know what they are doing" (Luke 23:34). Even when others do not ask us for forgiveness, God calls us to a spirit of forgiveness. So what do we do with someone in the public eye whose actions confuse all we have taught our children about honesty? If we continuously voice our attacks at the person, then soon our children will not be able to distinguish us from the media. In order to turn this confusion into an opportunity, talk honestly with your children about the mistakes the person has made, but do it with sorrow that he made them.

Do it with empathy. Demonstrating an empathetic spirit toward anyone whose actions anger you is much harder than lambasting him every time you become frustrated with all that has taken place. Watching you and listening to you during the frustrating times is when your child will see your true character and model it. Isn't it amazing that our children tend to choose our flaws to copy the most?

If you allow yourself to continue to openly condemn someone in front of your children, the impact of your words will lessen. They will begin to turn you off when you start your "speech."

Children want to be happy. They want to think happy thoughts and hear happy words. They feel safe when they do. They have to be taught to have a negative outlook. A child who constantly hears the negative will be trained to find the negative in others, in himself, and in his relationship with God.

When someone has done something wrong and you feel the need to discuss it with your family, or your children ask you about it, try following the suggestions from this dialogue:

Daughter: Mom, I heard some bad things at school about our neighbor, Mr. Ray.

Mom: Tell me what you heard, Sweetie.

Daughter: Some kids were saying he robbed the bank. Is that true?

Mom: I don't know every detail, but I will tell you what I read in the newspaper. Mr. Ray worked at the bank and he admitted that he did a wrong thing. He used some of the bank's money for his own use. The money really belongs to all the other people who have money in that bank.

Daughter: That's stealing. Will he go to jail?

Mom: I don't know how it will turn out. Yes, it is stealing. You might hear some adults use the word *embezzlement*.

Daughter: Didn't he know it was wrong?

Mom: We don't know what he was thinking or feeling. We do know that it is always wrong to steal. My heart goes out to his family. I know they are hurting and I believe he is hurting too.

Daughter: Chad told me that his father thought they ought to lock up Mr. Ray for a long, long time.

Mom: The court will decide what to do. He will have to face the consequences for what he has done. He was definitely wrong to do it. But instead of us concentrating on his wrong deed, let's think about how we can help his family. They will need someone who will still talk to them and support them. I am not sure that they go to church.

Daughter: We can pray for them.

Mom: Yes, we can pray for his family and for Mr. Ray. He will have to pay the consequences, but God is forgiving and He still loves Mr. Ray. That's why I don't really like to go around talking to other people about the bad things people do. I would rather spend my time praying that they would turn to God and allow Him to change their lives.

What did Mom do?

1. She made sure the daughter knew that what Mr. Ray did was wrong all the time.

2. She asked her daughter to tell her what she had heard so she could give clarification if needed. Children often believe everything their friends tell them. Teach your child to find out the facts.

3. She moved her daughter away from destructive criticism to constructive help. She could have agreed with Chad's father or she could have chosen to say something inflammatory about Chad's father, but instead she steered her daughter to the needs of the hurting family and to God's grace.

4. Through her speech, she demonstrated a spirit of forgiveness and empathy.

In his book *Victory Over the Darkness*, Neil Anderson offers 12 steps to forgiveness, emphasizing that until we forgive the person who has hurt us, we allow the person to continue to hurt us because we cannot release the past.

He offers these 12 steps to unchain us from the past and get on with life:

1. On a sheet of paper, write the names of those who have offended you. Write out a description of the sufferings their wrong has caused you.

2. After writing down how you feel about each person, face the hurt and the hate you feel. If we allow our emotions to lie buried, we will pass up the potential for forgiveness to occur.

3. Even though our heart would cry out that life isn't fair and there is no justice, we look to the cross of Christ.

4. Decide that you will not use the other person's sin against him in the future.

5. Forgiveness is a crisis of the will. Your primary concern is not how the other person behaves, but that you chose to forgive.

6. Pray and read off every name from your list. Tell God you forgive each person. If you have suffered from bitterness for several years, consider talking to a trusted counselor or friend.

7. Now, destroy the list. You are free! There is no need to tell those who offended you about your list. It was between you and God.

8. Your decision to forgive may or may not result in major changes in the other person's life. Pray that he will find freedom in your decision.

9. Try to understand those you have just forgiven. They are victims also.

10. Look for the positive results of forgiveness in yourself. After a period of time, you will be able to think about them without feeling resentment or hurt.

11. Take time to thank God for what you have learned about yourself and your relationship to others and to Him through this experience.

12. Be sure to accept your part of the blame for the pain you suffered. Admit it to God and others.[12]

The process of forgiveness is as much for ourselves as for the person we forgive. The underlying anger and hurt about the past can be very destructive to our current relationships. Admitting the pain and resolving the conflict through forgiveness are major steps toward honesty.

Cultivate a Forgiving Spirit in Your Child

If we are raising honest children, we help them cultivate a forgiving spirit. There is no better attribute they can learn from anyone than how to be honest with themselves and God so they will know when and how to forgive or ask for forgiveness, learn from it, and move on.

Values Check

I Lead, You Follow

You are a role model in demonstrating forgiveness. But you are also a role model as you admit to struggling with forgiveness.

- *Allow your children to know that you struggle in this area. Knowing this will help them understand that you are not perfect and accept the fact that no one is.*

- *Listen to what you are saying about someone else you haven't forgiven.*

- *Listen to what you are saying to them when you continue to pick on yourself for past mistakes. Claim the promise in Psalm 103.*

  > *"For as high as the heavens are above the earth, so great is His love for those who fear Him; as far as the east is from the west, so far has He removed our transgressions from us. As a father has compassion on his children, so the LORD has compassion on those who fear Him.*
  > *Psalm 103:11–13*

- *Ask God to show you people whom you have held a grudge against or people you need to go to and ask for forgiveness. Wipe the slate clean. As David said, "Create in me a pure heart, O God, and renew a steadfast spirit within me" (Psalm 51:10).*

- *Listen to your children when they seem hurt. Often, what seems so insignificant to us as adults is of vital importance to their feelings. Try to get inside your child's heart and feel what he is feeling.*

You and I Lead Together

Study the stories in the Bible that teach about forgiveness. Children are drawn to the adventure in the story of Joseph. Break the story into parts, so you can study each adventure with your child. The story of Joseph and his brothers is found in Genesis 37, 39, 40–50. Younger children will enjoy looking at pictures from a Bible storybook. But be sure to show every age child where it is found in the Bible so they will know it is not just a pretend story. Emphasize the spirit of forgiveness which Joseph showed to his brothers.

- *An excellent Bible study for you and your teenager is the life of David. Read through 1 and 2 Samuel and the first two chapters of 1 Kings. Make a time line charting the life of David. Look at how far-reaching his victories and his failures were. After reading 2 Samuel 11 and 12, read Psalm 51 to sense the repentant heart David had after he had sinned against God. He did not put the blame on anyone else; he came honestly before God and asked for forgiveness.*

- *As you watch TV and movies together, watch for situations you can discuss with your children in which characters did something wrong and needed to ask for forgiveness. Listen to your children's answers to discern what they understand and what they are confused about.*

- *When bad situations happen locally and nationally, talk about them as a family. This is the perfect opportunity to model empathy and think about what your family can do to help a bad situation become redemptive.*

- *Using kind words such as "please," "thank you," "excuse me," and "I'm sorry" will help your whole family develop a considerate spirit toward one another.*

- *When family squabbles occur (and they will!), don't let siblings and parents harbor anger and resentment. Talk about the situation openly with your children. Let each side discuss the situation using healthy family rules such as: no screaming or yelling at each other; no use of language to make the other person feel bad; never demonstrate retaliation through physical abuse of any kind; and allow others to speak.*

You Lead, I Follow

- *Praise your preschooler for saying kind words such as "I'm sorry" and "thank you."*

- *Praise your child when you hear him admit his mistakes and ask for forgiveness.*

- *Be alert to how often your child comes home from school and complains about how mean someone was to her. Perhaps she is the one who needs to work on forgiveness and honesty. If your child seems to be a gossiper, help her sort out if she is carrying a grudge against someone.*

- *Whenever your children or teenagers are "out of sorts," check your own barometer—perhaps you are adding to the problem. When your child thinks you do not love him enough to forgive him, then he will demonstrate those feelings in a way that may not be acceptable.*

The Bigger They Are, the Harder It Gets

Asking forgiveness is very humbling for anyone, anytime. When our children are young, they forgive us quickly and we can teach them to forgive. When your 5-year-old says, "Mommy, I'm sorry I spilled my milk on the carpet," you can model forgiveness by responding with, "Thank you for telling me. Let's clean it up. Please go get some towels." Unless your child is habitually spilling milk, this response is all it takes to help him learn how to forgive and to assure him of your continued love and trust.

As children grow, it can be more difficult to forgive and to model forgiveness. When our children are small and they say and do bad things, we are certain that nothing that "angelic" can really know what she is doing or saying. But when that same little angel grows a couple of feet taller and says and does the very same things, suddenly she doesn't look so angelic anymore. Because so much time, love, and money have been invested in her by the time she reaches adolescence, there is an internal parental barometer that expects more from her. At the same time, because you as a parent have also had time to mature over the years, your child expects more from you. It becomes a mutual accountability of trust and love.

On average, teenagers don't give parents as many chances as younger children do. If they sense they cannot trust you, they won't. If they sense you don't love them, they won't stick around to give you the chance. Have you seen teenagers with parents who can't forgive them? You know the kind—the parent who takes everything as a personal character attack and attacks back, or the parent who holds a grudge and withdraws from the teen.

What happens when a teen comes from a home where a parent has trouble forgiving?

- *The teen develops low self-esteem.*
- *The teen is unforgiving toward others.*
- *The teen will have difficulty relating to others and forming significant relationships because of the lack of trust.*
- *The teen rebels against his family and others in authority roles at church, at school, and in the community.*
- *The teen leaves home with extra baggage that was never dealt with. That baggage will follow him around for his entire adult life if he doesn't seek help facing it. He will pass on the baggage to the next generation even though it is too heavy for them to handle.*
- *The teen may have problems with a growing relationship with God because his views of God are so tied to his views of his parents.*

Let's look at it from the other side. What kind of influence does a forgiving parent have on a teenager?

- *The teen is more forgiving toward others.*
- *The teen is able to be honest about mistakes.*
- *The teen has more self-confidence and self-esteem.*
- *The teen trusts God because he knows he can trust his parents.*

One of the top fears parents have regarding forgiveness is that the teen will see it as smoothing over the wrong or even condoning the wrong. On the contrary, forgiveness never excuses emotionally or physically harmful behavior. When your teen hears you say, "You are forgiven," she is hearing that you acknowledge what she did, you accept her apology for it, and you still love her and accept her. She will understand that she can still trust you even when she has done something wrong.

Part of being a teenager is making mistakes. It's hard to be perfect at something you simply haven't had enough time to perfect yet. But often, parents love their teens for what they are and not who they are. Your home is a laboratory for your children and teens to find their way, to make mistakes, to find support, and to try again.

If you were the perfect teen when you were growing up, then you're in a very, very small club. It would help parents of teens to think back to their own teen years and to the mistakes that were made and the response of the parents involved. How did their response make you feel? If you start thinking your teen is making way too many mistakes, count your own first!

Keep in mind, the parent who acknowledges his mistakes and asks for forgiveness stands a much better chance of his children coming to him with their problems and mistakes. Why? Because the adult who is willing to ask for forgiveness is more likely to give it as well. And because the adult who doesn't set himself up as a perfectionist will attract those who know they aren't perfect.

Go against the Grain to Gain

Forgiveness is natural for God but unnatural for us. It steps on our toes and attacks our sense of justice. Where we used to think of forgiveness as a religious act, research now shows that forgiveness is needed for our mental, physical, and emotional well-being.

No matter how unhappy the problems at home may be or how broken the relationships are, forgiveness must be shared in order for healing to take place. You may be facing marital strife or living with children and teens who are out of control. Perhaps your family has become self-centered instead of Christ-centered.

Parents, for your children, you are God's representative. As you demonstrate love and forgiveness, discipline and faith, you can allow the very present love of Jesus Christ to shine through you and permeate the lives of your children.

⑧ HOPE

"It doesn't take much. Just a whisper. Just a wisp. Just a flicker. Just a word. Only one breath. Just a sigh. Just a glance. It doesn't take much … just a sprig of hope."[13]

These words speak to many of us today in a time of little hope. It is revealing that scientists tell us that rats without light (hope) drown in a jar of water in a little over 3 minutes. Yet when a glimmer of light (hope) is shown, the rats swim for more than 36 hours!

But just what is hope? Is it a philosophy or a state of mind or an emotion? Most of the current theories do not include hope as an emotion. But in earlier times in history, prior to the benefits of scientific knowledge and technology, hope was considered one of the most fundamental of all emotions. Although there are several definitions of hope, they all contain some common themes, including:

- *Hope involves some uncertainty of an outcome.*
- *Hope concerns matters of importance.*
- *Hope reflects a person's values.*

Someone said it is not the destination that matters, it is the journey that is important. Every step of the journey is indeed important, however, knowing the destination is of God serves to give long-lasting hope to the journey.

"For I know the plans I have for you," declares
the LORD, "plans to prosper you and not to harm
you, plans to give you hope and a future."
Jeremiah 29:11

When we are sure of our destination, the journey has meaning and purpose. If we are children of God and our destination is heaven, then we experience eternal life every day. Through the saving grace of Jesus Christ we have hope for the "by and by" and a purpose for the here and now.

You've read the final chapter of the Good News; you know how the book ends. What a marvelous gift from God! Because we do not have to worry about our destination, we can concentrate our hopes and energies on the journey. In Paul's letter to the Colossians he wrote, "We always thank God, the Father of our Lord Jesus Christ, when we pray for you, because we have heard of your faith in Christ Jesus and of the love you have for all the saints— the faith and the love that spring from the hope that is stored up for you in heaven and you have already heard about in the word of truth, the Gospel that has come to you" (Colossians 1:3–6a).

Word of the faith and the love for others that the Colossians demonstrated had reached Paul. Where did Paul say their love sprang from? It was an outward demonstration of their hope secured in their final destination.

At various times in life, children, teenagers, and adults long to know who they are and why they are here. Teach your children well. Share with them the blessed hope that will allow them to live out their faith in loving others with the same love God has for them.

A Personal Note

When our children are young, they are so bright-eyed and full of hope about what they want to become. I remember the night my 4-year-old Emily informed me that she wanted to be a ballerina. I affirmed her decision. A few minutes later she added that she wanted to be a doctor. I affirmed that decision also. A few more minutes went by and she proclaimed a calling to be a missionary. I chuckled at the combinations, all of which required hard work and determination.

My son wanted to be a paleontologist before he was old enough to spell the word and certainly before I was old enough to pronounce it! He remained committed to this goal for years. As a high school junior, he admitted he knew more about what he wanted to be when he was in fourth grade than he did as a junior.

Given affirmation and permission, a child will choose hope. If taught about a lasting hope in Christ, he stands a better chance of "making it" through adolescence to find the hope and zeal of a young adult.

Ellen

What Is Hope?

Hope is the expectancy and the excitement in faith. It is the confidence and joyful anticipation that what we believe will happen. Children will learn to be hopeful from watching and listening to you. Hope will strengthen your child's faith. Make hope part of her vocabulary by making sure it is part of yours. Give her permission to hope and to be excited and expectant.

Hope Is Learned

A series of comprehensive studies performed in 1990 by social constructivist James Averil concluded that hope includes learned behaviors and thought processes that are gained through the socialization process. The findings of the studies support the theory that hope is a culturally determined concept acquired by children during the language acquisition process of early childhood. The studies acknowledge a strong religious component to hope, and honesty is the beginning point. Honesty is the best policy but it can sometimes be difficult to hear. Hope allows us to believe that God will honor Himself through our honesty.

The studies go on to indicate that children are taught the concept of hope. They suggest there is no evidence that people actively think about whether it would be helpful or not to have hope in any situation. If a person is hopeful, it seems to just "kick in" to his outlook based on his earlier learning.

How exciting to think that as parents we can pass on to our children a hopeful way of approaching life. However, the converse statement is staggering. As parents, we can choose to just get the job done and never discern what attitudes our children are learning from us. We can consciously or unconsciously leave out hope.

Keep in mind that children learn hopefulness through our words, actions, and prayers.

Let them hear you:

- *Thank God for a new day to experience Him and all of creation.*
- *Offer words of encouragement and support to a friend with a problem or illness.*
- *Talk more about what's good in the world than what is bad.*
- *Make expectant plans for the future.*
- *Pray for help in tough situations.*
- *Say the word hope frequently.*

Let them watch you:

- *Try different ways to solve a problem without giving up.*
- *Go to God's Word for guidance and direction.*
- *Express hopefulness in your eyes and gestures as you talk to them and to others.*
- *Get excited and moved by what people say, by music, by children, by art, by nature, by God.*
- *Set goals and work toward accomplishing them.*

  Now faith is being sure of what we hope for and certain of what we do not see. Hebrews 11:1

Hope Is Tenacious

Webster's defines tenacious as "not easily pulled apart, cohesive, tough; persistent to maintaining or adhering to something valued as habitual."

Hope keeps on keeping on when we want to give up. Just like the Energizer Bunny, hope keeps on going and going and going. Maybe that's a good visual image for your children because hope gives us the energy to keep trying. Children who are taught hope know that "if at first you don't succeed, try, try again." Encourage your child to keep trying. If a good attempt is made, there is no failure. Praise your child when she shows fortitude and determination.

Hope is strong because it believes in the future. You have seen a time wall with clocks from time zones all over the world on it. That is a picture of hope. Hope encompasses what we trusted in the past and what we know in the present to keep us looking toward the future. Your children do not have a past of hope yet; they must depend on you to share yours with them. Tell them the stories of your faith when God sustained you through difficult times.

Hope copes. When the going gets tough, the hopeful do too. A hopeful person pulls from every positive resource to get through a tough situation. He understands that "this too shall pass" and hangs on, knowing a better day will come.

Teach your child what to do when she needs support. Surround her with people who encourage her and to whom she knows she can turn when she needs hope. Help her understand there is no honor in coping alone.

Hope breeds courage and confidence. A hopeful person is not afraid to press on. He knows that he has weathered storms in the past and that gives him confidence to make it now. Giving your child hope will give him the confidence to stand up against the odds. His expectancy will outweigh his fear.

Hope Is Optimistic

When the doctor comes out and says, "It was malignant," it is our hope in God's unlimited love and concern for us that helps us go on. When the press and everyone around you are blasting about the latest political controversy and declaring gloom and doom for the country, you are the one who says, "We can learn from this. All is not lost. There is still good in America." What does optimistic hope do for your family?

- *It helps put the emphasis on what you have and not what you don't have.*
- *It keeps you focused on your strengths while being honest about your weaknesses.*
- *It encourages positive thinking to solve family problems.*
- *It celebrates the successes of one another.*
- *It forgives mistakes and moves on.*
- *It makes plans to share hope with others in need.*
- *It finds reason to laugh together even in tough times.*

Hope Is Healthful

Basically, hope is a mental process of feeling positive about yourself. When we lose hope, we feel trapped by our situation, and our self-esteem drops. When we lose hope, our mental and spiritual health and general well-being wane.

In 1997, the *American Heart Association Journal Report* cited a relationship between hopelessness and heart problems. A 4-year study of 942 middle-aged men links hopelessness to a faster progression of atherosclerosis, in which artery narrowing occurs and the risk of heart attack or stroke is increased. The study defined hopelessness as feeling like a failure or having an uncertain future. Those who reported experiencing high levels of hopelessness had a 20 percent greater increase in atherosclerosis than those with lower levels. Susan Everson, Ph.D., of the Public Health Institute in Berkeley, lead author of the study, said, "This is the same magnitude of increased risk that one sees in comparing a pack-a-day smoker to a nonsmoker." Everson reports, "The take-home message is that physicians need to realize that hopelessness has a negative impact and adds to the burden of the disease." The evidence supports the belief that when a person gives up hope, it has adverse consequences on his mental and physical health.

Hope Is Compassionate

Our source of hope is the "God of the second chance." We take hope from the stories in the Bible about men and women who were given another chance to live out God's purpose for their lives. Great fathers of our faith such as Moses, David, and Abraham all made mistakes and were given an opportunity to begin again through grace and forgiveness with restored hope for the future.

- *When the report comes back malignant, God gives us hope.*
- *When we "blow it" with our child, God reminds us that there is another day to love again.*
- *When the bad report card is brought home, we can calmly talk about how to change the outcome in the next six weeks.*

- *When our 2-year-old has been in time-out five times in one day, we forgive and hug and start over the next day.*

No matter how big or small the problem or the child, God offers us hopeful compassion to begin again.

Values Check

I Lead, You Follow

There are many adults who grew up in homes filled with pessimism, anger, and even violence, who have consciously chosen to become parents of hope in order to create a different environment for their own children. As adults, we realize there are different ways to approach life. However, a child believes that his environment is the way everyone is growing up. He does not yet know there is another choice. Infuse him with our hope in Christ which brings hope for each day.

What causes you to lose hope? Be aware of consistent negative feelings. How often do you feel anxious or depressed? How do you respond to challenging situations? Our lifestyle and our outlook on life are critical factors in our ability to control our levels of anger. When we harbor resentment and anger toward others, it affects everything we do with everyone else in our lives. To counteract negative feelings of defeat or insecurity, substitute more powerful, positive thoughts. "Finally, brothers, whatever is true, whatever is noble, whatever is right, whatever is pure, whatever is lovely, whatever is admirable—if anything is excellent or praiseworthy— think about such things," St. Paul counsels us in Philippians 4:8. Gradually, the more powerful thoughts will suffocate the negative ones and your hopeful way of living will become habitual. To help with hope:

- *Read the Bible and inspirational writers who tell stories of God's love for us in Jesus.*

- *Read books that make you laugh; books that focus on the joy we have in Christ.*

- *Find positive experiences in your family history to celebrate.*

- *Honestly examine your heart. What keeps you from accepting hope?*

- *Study the following Scriptures and ask God to strengthen you and give you hope: Jeremiah 29:11, Psalm 42:5, Psalm 62:5, Psalm 119:74, Psalm 130, Psalm 147:11, Proverbs 13:12, Isaiah 40:31, Romans 12:12, 1 Thessalonians 1:3, 1 John 3:3.*

- *Think of three projects or goals you want to accomplish this year. Write them down. Decide the order in which you want to accomplish them. Allow yourself to dream about them and think toward their completion. Use this as a starting point for setting worthwhile goals that give positive direction to your life.*

- *Seek friendships with those who have a hopeful, optimistic outlook on life. Avoid individuals who encourage self-pity.*

- *Welcome new ideas.*

- *Don't take yourself too seriously. Instead, develop a healthy sense of humor and lightheartedness.*

- *Learn from others.*

You and I Lead Together

We have a choice about how we think and act. Helping your child begin to take responsibility for her thoughts and actions will build her self-confidence and allow her to hope. Giving hope means that even when being disciplined, a child realizes he has value.

A Hopeful Scenario

Dad: Hey, Son, let's talk for a minute about what happened at school today. Tell me what you did.

Son: I hit another kid because he pushed me down.

Dad: Son, is that something we go around doing?

Son: No, Sir.

Dad: Tell me what you could have done instead.

Son: I could have walked away or told a teacher.

Dad: If you had, what might have happened?

Son: Well, some kids might have laughed at me, but I wouldn't have gotten in trouble.

Dad: You're right. That would have been a tough decision. Whose choice was it?

Son: Mine.

Dad: What can you do if this happens again?

Son: Try to walk away, or tell someone he hit me.

Dad: Good idea. You know that fighting is wrong and is only an easy way of expressing your anger, but then you are still angry and get in trouble on top of it. In our family, we have established a rule: no fighting. You broke the rule and will have to pay the consequences. Do you understand, Son, that it was your choice to break the rule and suffer the consequences?

Son: Yes, Dad.

Dad: Son, I love you, but I don't love what you did. If you choose to fight again, we will have to talk again. Now, this is over. Tell me something good that happened at school today.

What does this scenario give to the child?

- *An understanding that he made a wrong choice*
- *An opportunity to reflect on (to be sorry for) his actions*
- *A chance for the child to create a better solution for next time*
- *The assurance that even though the father was not happy with the son's actions, the son was forgiven and could move on*
- *A hopeful spirit demonstrated by a dad who assured his son of his unconditional love, reflecting God's forgiving love in Christ*

Even when you must discipline your child, it is possible to do so in a way that promotes hope:

- *Use a calm voice.*
- *Use questions and statements that place responsibility for the actions directly on the child.*
- *Help the child articulate ways he can make a better choice next time.*
- *Forgive him.*

Providing hope to your child is like giving her a new pair of glasses. It provides her with another outlook. A child who possesses hope learns that good can sometimes come from tough situations. For example:

- *When your family must move to a new town:*

  Hopeless—"I don't want to move! I'll lose all my friends."

Hopeful—"I'm going to miss my friends, but I know I can make some new ones."

Hopeless—"I had my room fixed just the way I wanted it."

Hopeful—"Mom let me pick between two rooms, and I got the one I wanted."

- *When your child feels rejected:*

  Hopeless—"I was picked for the all-star team, but I didn't get to play."

  Hopeful—"I was the youngest player on the team. Next year I'll be older and bigger and faster."

  Hopeless—"I failed the test again. Mom's going to kill me."

  Hopeful—"I can't believe it. Dad failed his driving test three times. Maybe there's hope for me!"

- *When your teen starts to think about dating:*

  Hopeless—"He will never ask me out."

  Hopeful—"I'll see if he wants to go out with a group of us."

  Hopeless—"I want to ask her to go out with the other couples, but I don't have any cash."

  Hopeful—"What if the guys cook burgers at my house and we split the rental on some movies?"

- *A best friend moves away:*

  Hopeless—"I won't get to see her until Christmas holidays."

  Hopeful—"We could e-mail every day."

Hopeless—"She's going to find a new friend and forget me."

Hopeful—"We will always be close, but I am glad I have other friends that I care about too."

Keep in mind that kids feel hopeful when:

- *They understand they have value.*
- *They know you value them.*
- *No matter the situation, they can count on you to listen to them.*
- *You will take time to put everything else aside to help them.*
- *They remember or you remind them of times in the past when they made good decisions.*
- *They see hope in the world around them.*
- *They grow in understanding and trust in the hope of eternal life with God.*

Natural Hope

Use nature to give your children hope. Point out the changes in seasons. Plant seeds and watch them grow over time. Learn the constellations together. Study the migration and feeding patterns of birds. Learning about the wonders of nature will affect your child's hopeful spirit. Children will equate God's care for nature with His care for them.

A Personal Note

I call it Hummer Hope. If you are a bird watcher, you will automatically identify. Along with my parents and several "hummer friends," we start anticipating the arrival of our "little buddies" in early summer. Each year, we put out our feeders (accented with red) and plant special gardens to attract the smallest of all birds, the hummingbird. Hummers are remarkable. North America's smallest hummingbird weighs little more than a dime.

With near-invisible wings that beat 60 times a second, their average flight speed is 25 to 30 miles an hour with an average heart rate of 1,260 beats a minute. The hummingbird's nest is no bigger than a walnut shell and is made from spider webs and plant down.

You would think an alien space ship had landed when the hummers appear. The phone lines stay busy reporting the first sighting to hummer friends. It is a race to see who spies the first one each season. By late summer, we find the hummers more at home around us and much more brave. They flit all around us when we go outside. Early morning and evening is my favorite time of day to observe them. I marvel at their speed and abilities. I marvel at their tenacity. They must chase off each other, bees, and wasps to get to the feeder and drink the nectar.

They give no warning when they will pack up and head south for the winter. I just notice that their feeder is not emptying anymore and after a few days I miss seeing them.

Why do so many people enjoy the little creatures? To me, they bring hope. I anticipate their arrival each year and, as I watch them, my own spirit is bolstered. If the "little buddies" survive, so can I. If God can make something so tiny, yet so vivid and speedy, He surely made and cares for me. I have tiny worship experiences with a big God when I observe the intricate detail of His handiwork.

When my hope seems to dim and waver, I think of the hummer and gain the strength to continue with the journey.

Ellen

Lemons or Lemonade?

If it were up to the media, your children would see or hear very little positive information that would give them hope. Counter the reports of a "doom and gloom" media and negative people by offering hope to others. As your family participates in ministry projects to others, their lives are changed and they have hope. Hope is contagious. When you give it away, it will increase within you and within your child. Focus family efforts on ways to serve God and help others in practical ways.

You Lead, I Follow

Few things are as gratifying and humbling as when your child or teenager reminds you to cheer up and not lose hope. It is at that moment you know they listened.

Our children hope with such enthusiasm and energy, though often with impatience. Be invigorated by your child's hopeful spirit. Thank God when you see hope demonstrated in his life. Express to your child or teen how much it encourages you when he is hopeful. Resist the urge to control his hopeful energy. Allow him to experience his own hope without having to make it yours. It will prepare him for times when he must rely on himself for courage and strength.

Soaring Hope

> "But those who hope in the LORD will renew their strength. They will soar on wings like eagles; they will run and not grow weary, they will walk and not be faint." Isaiah 40:31

Keep in mind that no matter how tumultuous life gets, Christians live by hope. The student about to flunk a course keeps struggling and will do her best, as long as there is hope. The husband or wife who has been unfaithful yet repents asks simply but poignantly, "Forgive me and give me just one more chance." And that really means, "I'll give my all if there is just one glimmer of hope." The alcoholic who has seen despair at its worst and has been the carrier of despair to countless other people, when he becomes determined, only asks for "one day or one hour or one minute." All he really wants is the possibility that he can make it. With hope, he tries.

If you've ever felt despair or been depressed, you know full well that it's the faint breaking in of light that says, "Yes, there is hope." Things can be better! You can make it. Life does have promise.

Regardless of the circumstances in your family, no matter what experiences brought you to where you are, no one can stop you from thinking positively except yourself. God promises His strength to those who put their hope in Him. With His help, we decide we are going to take personal responsibility for our lives. Hopeful living leaves little time and energy for self-pity, depression, and wrong attitudes.

The bottom line is other people will disappoint us. Our family and friends will let us down. There is no real security except in God. And the more we trust in Him, the more we are free from worry and free to hope. Without hope, we have to interpret every challenge with less than desired results as a failure. However, with hope there is no failure, only obstacles we can learn from before moving on.

A Wake-Up Call

Perhaps political events in the last few years are just the wake-up call we all need. There is no better time than right now to

- *Pray to God about your family's needs and listen to the response.*
- *Ask for forgiveness from the hurts and wounds of the past.*
- *Rejoice that Jesus Christ is in the very heart of your home, to give you comfort, strength, and a new sense of purpose for your family.*

As you begin to teach the eight values outlined in this book, the blessings you will receive as a stronger family will continue for generations to come. Yes, it is time to come home again … to the family!

6 6 6

1 President William Jefferson Clinton, State of the Union Address, 1994.

2 Pulsefinder On-Campus Market Study released by Greenfield Online, Inc., 1998.

3 Josh McDowell. *Right from Wrong*. (Nashville, Tennessee: Word Publishing, 1994) pages 8–10. All rights reserved.

4 Richard Capen. *Finish Strong*. (San Francisco, California: Harper Collins, 1996) page 65.

5 Stephen R. Covey. *The Seven Habits of Highly Effective People*. (New York: Fireside, 1990) page 128.

6 Dr. Grace Ketterman. *Preparing for Parenthood*. (Kansas City, Missouri: Beacon Hill Press, 1996) pages 21, 66.

7 Gary Smalley and John Trent. *Home Remedies*. (Portland, Oregon: Multnomah Press, 1991) pages 25–26.

8 Charlotte Erlandson and Sven Erlandson. "Fostering an Atmosphere of Respect and Honesty in the Home." *Parish Teacher*. May 1996, page 13.

9 Jeane Westin. *The Coming Parent Revolution*. (Chicago, Illinois: Rand, McNally, and Company, 1981) pages 188–89.

10 "Get Over It! Overcoming the Psychology of Victimization." Interview with Dr. Eric Dlugokinski. Media release by Pam McKeown, University of Oklahoma Health Sciences Center, 1996.

11 Win Arn, Editor. *The Pastor's Church Growth Handbook*. (Pasadena, California: Church Growth Press, 1979) page 29.

12 Neil T. Anderson. *Victory Over the Darkness*. (Ventura, California: Gospel Light/Regal Books, 1990) pages 203–205. Used by permission.

13 "A Sprig of Hope." Sermon given by Reverend Dr. Robert Young. Duke University Chapel, Durham, North Carolina, 1977.